TECHNIQUES TO AWAKEN YOUR 'SUPERMIND'

It is now agreed in the highest scientific circles that many people are capable of using their psychic energy in one way or another, though they may be totally unaware of the fact.

HOW TO BE MORE PSYCHIC is a straightforward do-it-yourself guide whose intent is to stimulate you to explore these powers for yourself, as a means to greater happiness, effectiveness and self-knowledge. According to the author, a practising psychic of many years' experience and a well-known discoverer and researcher of so-called 'supernatural' phenomena, the time is ripe for ordinary men and women to look upon these latent powers as functioning parts of their bodies, like the brain, the limbs and the muscles.

In this astonishing work, he tells you how to begin to discover the amazing potential of *your* psychic energy-store – and how to use it for your own and others' benefit.

How To Be More Psychic

IVOR POWELL

SPHERE BOOKS LIMITED
30/32 Gray's Inn Road, London WC1X 8JL

First published in Great Britain by
Neville Spearman Ltd 1977

Copyright © Ivor Powell 1977

First Sphere Books edition 1979

Set in Intertype Times

Printed in Great Britain by
Cox & Wyman Ltd,
London, Reading and Fakenham

Contents

. . .what we call matter and force are but different manifestations of a single and infinite Unknown Reality.

Lafcadio Hearn.

It must strike most people, if the conditions are favourable, that they do not awake from sleep as if out of a nothingness, but as if they emerge from a rich but much lighter and more ethereal weaving and living encountered during waking hours to – sleep. It will certainly have struck many people, on waking, that during sleep they lived in an element where they felt themselves to be actually cleverer than when they were awake. . . For he was with his whole being – of this one must be clear – . . . but it cannot be grasped by this physical consciousness, and is generally forgotten at the moment of waking.

Rudolf Steiner.

What is Psychic?

Man feels inexplicable powers within himself and the Universe. It is in his nature to discover what this power is, to explain it as best he can in the terminology of a culture and an epoch, and to use it.

Although many people have always seemed incapable of perceiving or reacting to this power, many more are naturally 'psychic' from childhood. Some develop the gift steadily in one way or another, some have phases of attunement, while in some the capacity atrophies and fades after a more or less brief flowering. The abilities of psychism may suddenly appear and as suddenly vanish, and in spite of some interesting theories there seem to be no rules we know of to account for it.

Although the psychic is often described as 'mumbo jumbo' what it really means is 'waiting to be grasped'. And nobody, as yet, has grasped what it is all about, because it is an uncomfortable alien in the presence of respectable scientific and philosophical structures, silently rebuking them. This continues to be an intellectually embarrassing situation at the time of writing, but one for which the author makes no apology, and optimistically hopes for progress within the next few decades.

Education, the dreary handmaid of authority, persists in nurturing the intellect prior to the imagination and intuition. Yet the child in whom the former qualities have been encouraged may turn out a solid little *bon bourgeois*, and other whose upbringing is rooted in a pedestrian stolidity may unaccountably rise up and demonstrate that man is much more than he appears to be!

Although material slums are gradually disappearing from the planet, spiritual and cultural slums remain. But somehow the human race continues to dream, to look beyond the limits of self and a soulless environment, to aspire and to think in terms of the miraculous.

What is the psychic? What is psychism? In brief, any kind of perception that does not appear to depend on the physical organs of sense may be called psychism. And any phenomenon lying outside the present capacity of biology or physics to explain it may be called a psychic phenomenon. The psychic is part of man and nature, and yet has something to do with dimensions inherent in man and the Universe about which we know little. The intellectual powers are as remarkable as those more mysterious; reliance on the former to the exclusion of the latter, or vice versa, has been the greatest hindrance in the advancement of knowledge. With regard to the psychic, scientists today are still like primitive doctors who knew something of anatomy without knowing about the circulation of the blood; of cartographers who drew the map of the world without the Americas.

As our dread of being imposed upon by superstition abates in the slowly growing light of knowledge, we shall be able more clearly to understand what was meant by Sir James Jeans, an Astronomer Royal earlier this century, when he wrote that there would be no further significant advancement until the exploration of areas hitherto reserved as religious, spiritual or metaphysical.

The philosophic and scientific system which eventually grasps that there is no dichotomy between matter and spirit (although there may be clearly observable tensions and conflicts between them) and discovers the laws of their correspondence and interpenetration, will be, quite simply, master of the world and its destinies. Sensitives and aethereals who quail at such a prospect need feel no alarm, for such a system cannot come into being without an exceptionally high standard of development among its adepts.

Man is a being existing on several frequencies simultaneously. The so-called spirit or astral world, ghostly visitations, the vagaries of the seance and the ouija board, do not concern us in these pages. We are concerned with developing our personal, 'magnetic' psychism, and will find that one or other of its manifestations can mostly likely be improved with practice, like playing the piano or speaking a foreign language. More people are psychically aware than is generally believed. Until attention is drawn to the fact that they possess this awareness some may take their gifts for granted while others may even dislike drawing attention to them.

There ought to be neither superstitious dread nor sensationalism attached to psychic healing, clairvoyance, divination, prophecy, or dowsing, in all their various forms.

The Russians have proved that eighty per cent of people are capable of dowsing, but when most laymen watch a dowser at work with map and pendulum, or striding across country with the divining rods: or see the practitioner of radionics or radiaesthesia diagnosing or curing disease: or learn some general ideas related to homeopathic medicine or the herbal healing system devised by the late Doctor Edward Bach, the resulting incredulity is not surprising considering the scientific and philosophical atmosphere in which the modern world has developed. When the same laymen are informed that an aura – a force-field of varying hue and intensity – surrounds all living things: or that future action may be known or usefully influenced by consulting some form of oracle depending on certain arrangements of numbers, symbols or patterns, it is no wonder, given the intellectual background of our era, that incredulity mingles with contempt.

A science which sets a limit on consciousness and a system of thought unable to open itself to the marvels of universal being are of no service to humanity. Nevertheless, all forms of what the Russians admirably describe as psycho-biology are often inefficient in producing the results they set out to obtain. It may be that inconsistency of result is a built-in factor of psychic activity. It is more certain that the mists surrounding these highly charged frontiers of consciousness are in part due to long neglect, to the siphoning-off during many centuries of man's mental powers to other areas of reflection and activity.

It is astonishing that any consistent results are obtainable at all; the smallest result must convince that the human entity is much more complex than it appears to be. Yet it is essential for the beginner to be wary: nothing is more open to delusion and self-deception. The clairvoyant soon learns what a barrier to perception the subjective imagination can be. Every dowser knows how the ego and the pedestrian reasoning faculty can stand between himself and his goal. The spiritualistic medium has to learn to distinguish authentic communication from the phantoms that lumber out of the shadowy shunting yards of the mind!

A cheerful admission of our ignorance is a good start to psychic work. We have to be as honest as we are able and freely admit that we can make mistakes, as so few of us are instruments refined to perfection!

On the other hand, the work is ill-served by diffidence and lack of self-confidence.

Hesitations on the threshold of enquiry into psychic matters are sometimes caused by a belief that these things are the preserve of wild eccentrics, somehow inferior to their more solidly-based and worldly-wise fellows. A glance at the qualifications of the men and women, from Paracelsus onward, who have become absorbed in unconventional scientific systems, will be enough to reassure those in doubt. Rudolf Steiner, who had enough professional qualifications to have earned a Nobel Prize had he worked in an approved field, said that modern science knows as much about the human body as someone whose only knowledge of a calf is a veal cutlet on a plate. Dr. Edward Bach earned the derision of the medical establishment by giving up a highly paid and prestigious career in bacteriology to wander about in the Welsh woods, sometimes only with enough money to buy bread and cheese for himself and his dog. Sigmund Freud, near the end of his life, wrote that had he his time again, he would have devoted much more of it to psychic studies. Wilhelm Reich, who could have revolutionised the whole of Science – and revitalised mankind – was murdered by the C.I.A.

Napoleon believed in the strange imponderables of existence to such an extent that he said 'I would rather have a lucky general than a clever general'. Psychism can be like fairy gold – try to grasp it and it turns to a handful of dust. I do not say that more objective research and discovery are not possible. On the contrary. But the right conditions and the right attitudes have to be postulated before anything can be done. The cold intellectual approach will overlook the microscopically subtle mainsprings of much psychic activity, and will have to be 'warmed-up'; psychism does not fit in with the vocables of the thesis scribbler. Before further progress can be made in worthwhile discovery, it may be as well to remember an ingredient, essential in the discoverer, touched on in a sublime way by Wordsworth:

> . . .that serene and blessed mood,
> In which the affections gently lead us on, –

Until, the breath of this corporeal frame
And even the motion of our human blood
Almost suspended, we are laid asleep
In body, and become a living soul:
While with an eye made quiet by the power
Of harmony, and the deep power of joy,
We see into the life of things.

In psychic activity or research, our first efforts must be directed at discovering and examining our personal reality. A sustained interest in any area of psychism should tend to waken our whole being, although if an interest in such matters is simply a form of escapism, then the end result will be further withdrawal from the data of existence and neuroses will advance unchecked.

Continuous psychic effort does make heavy demands and is productive of specific stresses of a physical or mental order. To combat them, much quiet, meditation and a healthy way of life are of great assistance. In his fascinating books about a certain type of illumination and initiation in Mexico, Carlos Castaneda reports the wise man, Don Juan, as continually telling him to 'still the inner dialogue' – a helpful guide-line for anyone embarking on psychic work. Our minds are inclined, as are our five senses, to wander aimlessly, wool-gathering, running off at a tangent, shuffling hopes and fears back and forth without positive conse-quence. Nothing is more dulling to the vital force which activates our totality: a force available to us all because present in us all.

If dormant, this force can be roused, sometimes by enthusiastic interest alone, sometimes by enthusiasm plus a well-directed concentration. Such a concentrating process does not mean a tensing of the mental or other muscles – rather the reverse, indeed. The very fact that you are reading these pages with a degree of attention means you are capable of some form of development. It is simply a question of the direction recom-mended by your personal qualities. Your vital force may be mis-routing because of neurotic or psychosomatic conditions, in which case you can only wait and work for change and healing.

Through centuries of mismanagement of the human entity by Church and State the psyche has suffered great damage. All the human impulses have been warped by unbearable constraints. This is not a plea for a delirious libertarian outlook. The struggle for 'freedom' can become as negating and tyrannical as a highly prescriptive social structure. Man requires to know his situation, gauge his needs, and discover himself as both individual and social being with the obligations these incur.

A writer and poet, Robert Graves, and an occultist, Richard Gardner, have both pointed to the reinforced maleness of the past two millennia as a source of many ills besetting the human condition. Certainly, the world as it is at the present time seems to be the outcome of serious imbalances having their origin in the human mind. The ills of the world, and of man himself, may be summed up in one banal-sounding phrase: lack of love. No religion, government, work (especially psychic work) will bring enduring benefit unless it be based on the first of the Gospel messages: 'Good will Toward Mankind', with its sequent commandment 'Love One Another'. With benevolence and love creating the right conditions for clarity of thought, the world can be transformed, even at the eleventh hour.

However, this small book is not aimed at the great heights, but at modest pastures easily accessible to all. In describing some techniques of interpretation, in looking at aspects of dream and symbol, I have not hesitated to bring out old friends, time-honoured interpretations and means of divination whose greatest recommendation is their simplicity.

The discreet sage and self-effacing initiate know what is hocus-pocus and what is not. Most of us have not yet attained that state of enlightenment and so ought to keep things simple. Our capacity for the marvellous will not be diminished if we limit ourselves to small goals. With them, let us at first, and perhaps for a long time, be content.

Over-eager learners (like the young person who wrote to me 'I want to get into astral travel as soon as possible') are inclined to rush in where angels fear to tread. It may be true that to dare is the secret of magic, but it is best to avoid unprepared confrontations with the monsters lurking in our depths. To use alchemical language, the lion will not lie down with the lamb until the lamb is ready for the experience!

To de-mystify for the sake of clarity of thought and intellectual honesty, while at the same time preserving the sense of mystery, partly because it is beautiful and partly because that sense is an actual fertiliser of the psyche, is one of the most delicate problems we need to solve. In different cultural and historical contexts, people took their personal 'magnetic' psychism for granted. Their imagination was keener than ours, their consciousness, less exercised by the demands of a technological way of life, was capable of reaching greater depths and forming a type of reality far removed from the silliness and shallowness which characterise our epoch. In trying out some of the techniques of our forbears in full awareness of what we are up to, we may be able to discover some of the rich savour of being that is our birthright on this lovely planet.

One: Wake Up!

In the fairy tale of Jack and the Beanstalk, Idle Jack was not so idle after all, for he had the will to climb and the curiosity to find out what was at the top.

Most of us have not developed our intuitive, or psychic powers because we have not thought it possible. We often cannot recall our dreams because we are scared of them, or may not have made the effort. To play the piano, paint a picture or sing a song it is necessary to practise. This may not lead to concerts at the Albert Hall or critical acclaim, but if we try hard enough we inevitably produce something of worth. This is as true of the intuition as of anything else.

For development of the hidden faculties, some organisation is necessary, but there is no need to sit cross-legged on a mat in a shrine. You can get ahead as you get on with the business of daily life, unless your daily life so obsesses you that you have no time for anything else, when you may as well close this book here and now. You have to take a good look at yourself, and draw yourself together. Most of us are all over the place, wasting mental and physical energy. We permit our senses to be wrung out in a tide of triviality, our thoughts to run hither and thither like sheep demented by a stray dog.

To help along the 'drawing together' process, a little time spent daily on deep, concentrated breathing is the best thing we can do.

Sitting or standing erect without stiffness, the chin slightly lowered so that the head is a little forward, take a good, deep breath through the nostrils, filling the diaphragm to the count of three. Hold the breath to a count of three and expel through the open mouth to a count of three. Do this seven times. It steadies the pulse, regulates the heartbeat and calms the mind. Repeat as many times daily as conveniently possible.

When we are assailed by uncertainty and all the other storms which beset us, of 'mind, body and estate', productive inner development becomes difficult. When the storms seem to get beyond control, physical and mental ills appear. We can all help ourselves to a greater or lesser extent by reinforcing the breathing exercise with simple meditation. On the lines of what was once called 'positive thinking' this kind of meditation can be usefully employed by anyone of any religious or philosophical belief, or none. It is not intended to lead us into Nirvana, unless Nirvana consists in achieving wholeness of being. That is what we are trying for.

Our meditation should go something like this:

'My reality does not consist of these stresses which are weighing me down and wearing me out. I take full responsibility for their existence, but they are a very small part of the totality of my landscape. 'The real, greater, stronger, better "Me" is now stepping aside from this troubled area, and is taking comfort, nourishment and energy from the Universe. All about me there are great reservoirs of energy and power.

'I am draining away all the stagnant, muddied water which has filled me, and now I am letting in a fresh, bubbling tide of crystal water from the ever-brimming fount of life itself.

'Through my fingers, through my toes, through the top of my head, through the pores of my skin, I am absorbing Universal Energy.'

This kind of meditation needs a little time of quiet, perhaps preceded by some music, a few minutes of solitude, or the harmonious company of those with whom we are attuned. Only when consciousness is raised, the 'X' energy restored, and tensions are to some extent released, can we expect to make progress in psychic work. However, an easy life, free of care and obligation, does not seem to favour psychic work. It is the way we learn to evolve, through and because of strenuous often painful, involvement in existence, which wakens us up, and eventually teaches us the Unity of all.

We may or may not get the experience of One-ness or other interior illuminations. They are neither occasions for self-congratulation nor belief that they are a sign of some great inner advancement. They are simply a perception of a certain reality, and if we get no such agreeable interludes there is no cause to stop trudging doggedly ahead. Psychic development is as much a humdrum occupation as practising the scales. If the morning mail is delivered before you get out of bed, a good exercise is to lie quietly for a few minutes and try to 'see' if there are any letters in the box. At first, just go for a 'yes' or 'no' result. If you find yourself getting good at this, you might grow a little more ambitious and see (or 'guess') how many letters there are, or even what they look like.

Another good exercise is to open an envelope, take out the letter without looking at it and then 'see', or 'guess', what it is about. I often try people who have never done psychometry before (holding an object and making guesses about it is called psychometry) and many of them come up with something interesting. A very down-to-earth business man, the least 'mystic' person you could meet, was given a folded letter with a beautifully printed letterhead of a country house. After a couple of minutes he said 'This is a lot of nonsense! I just keep getting in my mind a picture of a big house in the country' and then described the picture of the house quite accurately. Next he was given a letter from someone in prison. He said 'All I can see here is a long number.'

Psychometry does not usually work in a place which is at all noisy and where there is a strong light. There is much discussion among practitioners of forms of psychism about the points of the compass and whether it is better to face one or other of them. Each novice will find out which is best for himself. It may matter a great deal, or not at all. But quiet and dimness do seem indispensable for psychometry.

With the above conditions in mind, try it with a friend, each having a few things with a known history of which the other person is ignorant. It is no good making a party game of it, as more than two people seem to inhibit the flow of communication. Psychometry is a most useful psychic activity, and is sometimes used by the police who ask a psychometrist to work with some object belonging to someone they want to know more about. Metal or leather which have been worn close to the skin for a long time (don't ask me how long a long time is – let us say a year or more if possible!) seem to give the best results, although many years since I received some strong impressions from an old coat which was sent me by Monsieur Jacques Locard of the Lyons police laboratories. For myself, I most enjoy using psychometry with antiques or reputed antiques. Fakes give a blank feeling; the real thing sends images and tingles through the mind, often a bit confused but enough to know the object is 'right'.

If you daily go into a building where there are several lifts in a row, every time you wait for a lift you might try guessing which one will be the first to arrive. If you have to catch a certain bus or train at a stop where they all go to different places, try to see how often you are right in predicting whether the next one will be yours or not.

Such faculties are best improved in quietness and a soothing atmosphere. You have to allow signals to go to the brain as spontaneously as possible, yet of course you have to know what you are trying to achieve. This is by no means easy. Once I was on the ground floor of a building with a friend, waiting for the lift. When it didn't arrive, we decided to walk up the wide, old-fashioned staircase. 'Which floor is it stuck on?' I asked. 'Fourth' he replied without hesitation. I tried my 'guess' but somehow in that fraction of time it had become laboured. 'Er – sixth' I ventured. Of course I was wrong and he was right.

'Seeing' and 'guessing' happen to different people in different ways. It may be that only an impression is felt, not necessarily a strong one. It may be a swiftly spontaneous verbal response which at first is surprising to the speaker until he or she gets used to it. 'Seeing' is usually a picture of some kind, but certain people only get a description like a moving tape with words written on it.

Prophetic intuitions or visions of a precognitive kind may occur in dreams, and we shall deal with these in another chapter. The kind of vision seen with the eyes, or is thought to be seen with the eyes, involves some complex psychological and neuro-pathological issues. What exactly is an 'eidetic image' or an hallucination? Nobody has yet explained either satisfactorily, and this is not the place to try.

Psychic development above all begins with the cultivation of AWARENESS. And not only of the present, but also the past. Development of memory is absolutely a *sine qua non* if psychic energy is to flow. People who are unaware find it hard to understand that there are people who are aware, and *vice versa*. You walk down a street each day. How much of it do you take in? How many of the buildings have you noticed? Are there any trees and what do they look like? Do you see how the sky and the light change? Do you notice the textures of road surface and pavement when wet or dry? Have you observed any of the individuals who go about their business there? Have you ever noticed that fern, timidly and gracefully – yet with such determination – growing out of a cranny in the parapet of the old wall whose history you may or may not have asked yourself?

But, you reply, you are a very observant person. You are very aware. If you weren't, how could you keep your job, drive your car? Well, such things may start out by demanding awareness, and then I am afraid they often become mechanical routines, growing in upon themselves. More of us suffer from ingrowing psyches than ingrowing toenails. So many of our fellow humans go about like zombies, shut up in their egos as though in a sack. How much they miss! How much they will never learn! The senses, the reason, the intellect, exist for these purposes and if they are unused the whole person stultifies. Wakefulness and awareness are all very well, but what if they are unaccompanied by the capacity to make an effort of the attention?

With the word 'attention', things become a little harder. 'Pay attention' is one of the earliest commands heard in the classroom, and how difficult it is to do so! To muster the attention, force should not be employed, or a reverse process is likely. A self-conscious effort of concentration produces muscular spasms but not much else. It is only necessary to watch someone absorbed in work, whether it be manual or intellectual, to see that concentration demands absorption in the subject, harmony with it and the self, and brings about an appearance of beauty and nobility in the whole scene.

In 'Zen In The Art of Archery' Eugen Herrigel writes of Japanese painters and flower arrangers in the Zen school. . . 'the Masters behave as if they were alone. They hardly condescend to give their pupils a glance, still less a word. They carry out the preliminary movements musingly and composedly, they efface themselves in the process of shaping and creating, and to both pupils and themselves it seems like a self-contained event from the first opening manoeuvres to the completed work.'

So, once more we come back to 'coming into oneself', – gathering up the scattered energies, stilling the distractions which take

21

us over so that we become passive instruments in a play of forces we have ourselves set up.

Aleister Crowley was to some extent an equivocal figure in the history of the occult sciences, but he was a remarkable man in many respects, his brilliance and erudition wasted through the insistence of an over-demanding ego. He employed a method of meditation which could also switch on the intuitive or clairvoyant powers, and the instrument he used was one of the hexagrams in the I Ching: the 'Chung Fu' (Inner Truth) no. 61 in Wilhelm's edition of the Book of Changes, the most ancient form of reasoned-out divination known to us.

The complex meanings assigned to this hexagram need not concern us here. Copied in red or black, and enlarged to a size congenial to the reader's taste, it forms a decorative and helpful adjunct for the student. Sit in a composed position for as long as the attention can be held without strain, which may not be more than two or three minutes or even less at first, looking into the centre of the hexagram. Keep the mind swept clear. Repeat daily if possible or as convenient. An improvement of the faculty of attention will come about, even if clairvoyance or intuition do not immediately surface.*

The reader may by now have remarked that I am trying to deal matter-of-factly with my subject. Most of us are great fantasists and nowhere more in the areas we are examining. Most human behaviour lacks clarity of intention. We will not get a clear view of psychism if we are dizzy with mystical experiences or the euphoria of the Unknown, or are bogged down in the fierce pseudo-scientific jargon often favoured by writers of a theosophic or quasi-religious turn of mind.

Genuine mystical experiences are to be highly valued; but it is also necessary to be sensible about them. And in these pages we are not dealing with the mystical but are exploring certain functions of the individual, group and universal mind. The laying down of hard and fast rules presents a difficulty. The traditional emblem of the psyche is the butterfly: a frail creature, not easily handled. Psychic capacities unfurl in a bewildering variety of ways. For some dowsers, the pendulum swings in one fashion, for others in quite a different manner. This clairvoyant may see things in symbols, that one in representational images. I have read a supposedly serious work on psychometry whose author describes to the budding seer the inner states and luminosities which may have accompanied his own development, but is not necessarily meaningful to anyone else's.

I know that if I am quiet and rested the signals improve in intensity. I meditate and perform various exercises, and also pray, partly because it has always been in my nature to do so, partly because I know that a certain way of living and direction of mind enhance my insights and increase my energy. There is no question of moral or spiritual superiority: if I were further advanced I would not need to do so much work on myself! But the fact is that since childhood I have been fascinated by the mysterious aspects of the Universe and our own selves, have always loved poetry and felt close to its sources, and find it easier to pray than to speak.

By prayer I do not mean addressing a deity or repeating formulae (though a formula may have a time-hallowed potency); for myself I believe prayer to be the heart's longing to partake more

---

* I am indebted for this unpublished information about Crowley to the late Tom Driberg.

fully of the essence of goodness, truth and beauty, the mind's desire to come to that which is highest (those sanctuaries on whose thresholds the keenest intellect must falter): and the soul's inborn inclination to commune with the Soul of the World.

Yoga is a universally-recommended vehicle for mental-psychic-physical development. For those who find one or other of the many types of yoga congenial there is nothing better. Those who do not easily adapt to the oriental culture-consciousness of Indian yoga should look elsewhere. There is plenty of choice, although certain techniques are simply yoga in a different guise. The technology of psychic work varies across the Earth as much as the expression of the religious instinct and the vocabulary of mysticism: yet all these variations possess linking features.

The false religiosity hawked down the centuries by self-interested hierarchies was seen by a great British genius, William Blake, for what it was. Of true religion he spoke thus:

'The Religions of all Nations are derived from each Nation's different reception of the Poetic Genius, which is everywhere call'd the Spirit of Prophecy.'

The Spirit of Prophecy is part of the spirit of man, leading an ordinary life and mixing with people in harmony and community. Wakening the psychic part of ourselves should not – and cannot if it is not to become a wretched delusion – be an exclusive preoccupation. True, special and intensified development of any sort demands isolation in conditions of psychological soundness, but a rarefied climate, self-imposed through vanity or a desire to escape or compensate, is the beginning of playing a role any wide-awake child will see through. We should develop our psychic awareness with and through others, with and through our conflicts and shortcomings in full consciousness of them.

And just how aware are we of the people we see each day? Do we sense their moods, do we know when they are unwell or sad? The expression, the eyes, the general posture, should all tell us something about our fellow beings. Even without being a palmist, it is possible to deduce a good deal about character from the hand. If we love and care for someone we learn all the changing manifestations of their feelings and respond to them. This is even true of the animals with which we come into contact. We sense their moods, just as they discern ours. Premonition and precognition are part of the natural equipment of consciousness, whether of man or beast or bird, and there is some evidence that plants possess it as well.

We can educate ourselves to fuller consciousness. We can urge that the education of children should take fuller account of their intuitive and perceptive potential. A more general realisation of this potential will affect every aspect of human activity and assist the growth process of the human race, at present uncertain of its directions and divided as to its aspirations, a state of affairs which cannot continue without the appearance of psychic-social maladies more serious than those which have caused the major problems of the world during the past two centuries. Let us hope that governments will in due course waste less of their treasure on fruitless and vainglorious projects, but spend largely on pursuing the study of total development in the human psyche. Each country should have its Ministry of Awareness and Fulfilment.

Yet nothing can be achieved without self-discipline. A young man who asked me to be his teacher was hurt when I refused. He pressed me for a reason and I told him 'I will teach you when you have learned to keep your room tidy.' To some, this may sound a trivial, bourgeois attitude, but it lies at the heart of what we are setting out to do.

Two: Dream and Reality

Our dreams are part of our reality. Many of us so neglect our inner life that we forget our dreams and only after careful recollection come to realise what we have been missing. It is certainly not easy to relate to dreams or to give them their proper significance.

Do not fear to dream! You may be a first-rate dreamer! Dreams are the instruments of the intuition, and you may have the capacity to know which of your dreams are meaningful and which reflect simply a drifting among the psychic wastelands surrounding all consciousness. Some dreams are a reaction on the sleeper of heat or cold, an upset stomach or an unexpected noise. We still know little about the mechanics of dreaming. It is possible that dreaming may be a continuous process, continually flowing even when we are awake and unaware of it. It is possible to dream while partially awake; instead of the dream taking place in a mansion of consciousness to which we gain access only during slumber, or in certain paranormal states, it can happen before the eyes, or so it seems.

The 'big' dreams so named by Jung, strong and clear, are not easily forgotten by anyone, although their meaning may not become immediately apparent. It is useful to keep a dream diary. If only dreams, which are themselves a record, could be precisely recorded and reproduced on film – but perhaps that would be a mixed blessing! A dream diary will soon begin to show that some dreams, or sequences of dreams, have a meaning related either to our mental state or daily life; others will have been caused by direct stimuli of a sensory nature, and others again will be only a jumble of images associated with immediate recollections and associations – the kind of dreams animals have.

Many of us have a much stronger psychic life, or stronger

psychic energy, untapped, than we care to admit. Yet it is through realisation of these energies that fear of the unknown may be dissipated. Once again, it may be necessary to repeat that by psychic life and energy nothing 'magical' or 'supernatural' is implied, for these are no more than the individual share of a sum total of conscious being and intention, interpenetrating with the material level of existence but often neglected by consciousness absorbed in the objectives of the latter.

Dreams prove that we have a real existence on planes of being other than that of daily life. In dreams we have often direct experience of those other realms, and from these we could learn that waking life is only part of the truth about ourselves. Certain dreams are perhaps not dreams at all, but the direct experience of astral travel, those times when, during sleep, we step out of our bodies and in our astral forms fly to the place of our desire, or attraction. Science will at last grow accustomed to the idea that this is not so extraordinary, and, if certain limited intellects quail at the prospect of the veil being lifted from the sanctuaries of knowledge, let the bolder spirits press forward with an increasing sense of responsibility and reverence for life.

Lucky and Unlucky Dreams

Dreams can solve with dramatic clarity a problem weighing on the dreamer. The symbols in which problem-solving dreams appear are usually special in the meaning they will have for the dreamer. Dream language often has characteristics as distinct as the work of one poet from another. The curious thing is that sometimes the dreamer himself fails to understand the symbols in which the dream formulates its message, and only later and later may be exasperated to discover what it was all about, too late.

The old dream almanacs have handed down interpretations which are often of the greatest antiquity, deserving respect for their powers of endurance if nothing else. Change of fortune for the good is traditionally presaged in any of the following ways.

Entering a large, well-built edifice and going upstairs or occupying an upper room.

Seeing people known to you standing round or above you

means that good fortune will attend your undertakings; to see them below you is not so good.

A good-tempered, amiable cat weaving its way through dreamland brings luck, but look out for deceptions if she is spiteful.

The sound of hammer on anvil brings great good fortune, so the old books tell us, but of course it is a sound many young folk will never have heard and would not recognise if they did, so it is probable that any brisk, constructive activity's concomitant noise would do as well.

Dreams of journeys indicate sound, steady progress in life; if the vehicle runs out of control beware of the passions, which are usually the cause of someone 'going off the rails'.

A happy wakening, encouraged and refreshed, seems to be no indication of what is to come. Many recorded cases exist of people who have slept soundly and woken at peace with the world while on the brink of disaster, or of sudden death. The contrary is also the case. Waking up depressed and disturbed with the feeling of having slept badly, haunted by unpleasant dreams, may mean nothing at all, and might herald good things.

Dreams of good things – gold, riches and bounty, often foretell the opposite. Jewels are usually thought of as bringers of happiness. Many people have their own special lucky or unlucky dreams, just as many of us have our private omens and feel that certain numbers or names are lucky or unlucky for us.

New Inventions

What dream diviner, sometime in the late 17th Century, thought up the generally accepted 'lucky' meaning for dreaming of drinking coffee? Was it that to dream of coffee, being then a luxurious and delicate commodity, indicated a state of mind not only appreciative of such things, but ready to work to get them?

How are we to interpret dreams featuring the telephone, television, or any other new invention which comes along with its mixed blessings? In these cases it is necessary to look for analogies in the areas of communication and entertainment, although, as in the case of all dreams, there may be special connotations for the individual.

Not so long ago, certain subjects were taboo in the western world. Nobody would ever have spoken about sex save in an indirect way, and thoughts and dreams about it were usually suppressed with anguished determination. Hence, the old dream books are almost silent about dreams having a frankly sexual content. Many are the old interpretations of dreams whose essence is evidently sexual, and the wise old diviners knew exactly what they might, and might not say to their querents. In our time, openness about many things has certainly widened the scope of dreaming, or at least of discussion about it; whether total candour is an improvement on the limitations of a generally-agreed hypocrisy remains to be seen.

Recurring Dreams

These may announce good or ill, may be prophetic, experienced again and again over many years, and often in an unexpected context will suddenly come true, and for reasons it may seem hard to explain. For example, a woman formerly living in Egypt had over many years a recurring dream that a negro child offered her a bouquet; when leaving the cemetery after her husband's funeral there happened to be a negro boy outside her villa, selling flowers, and he offered her a bouquet just as she left the car. Certain dreams need no recurrence to possess a fateful quality, forever impressed on the dreamer's memory. Such dreams have a haunting and terrible effect, yet may at last be seen to come true in a commonplace situation, and to have, after all, a banal meaning. Observation of the human organism, especially our own, demands a sense of humour; it is impossible that the Universe should lack the capacity to smile and crack a joke, and even at its darkest the human tragedy often has something comical about it.

Induced Dreams

Some drugs as well as hypnosis are able to effect changes in the consciousness, and may have an effect upon dreams. In ancient times, when hospitals were also temples, the priests knew how to induce healing dreams in their patients, usually figuring a vision of the god to whom the temple was dedicated. The invalid was put into a somnolent, receptive state, and was then 'given' the right vision. Quite how this was done we do not know; in the course of history man has lost as much as he has discovered. The ancients knew that much illness originates in parts of the organism still lying beyond the frontiers of our knowledge; these invisible portions of our totality can be healed by techniques still viewed by most doctors with suspicion.

Certain drugs are able to induce certain kinds of dream or vision. The famous 'water of Lethe' and 'water of Mnemosyne' used by the priests of the temple of Trophonius in Boetia, and the 'Ciceion', a draught given to the candidates for initiation at Eleusis, were no doubt of this type. Carefully supervised fasting and diet also have an effect upon the psyche, and hence on the dream-state, as the people of ancient times well knew. The *One Thousand Nights And a Night* (Alf Laila Wa Lail) has references to magical potions and perfumes, while the effects of opium and other narcotics are only too well known to many of our contemporaries.

Hassan Saba, 'the Old Man of the Mountains' who founded the Assassins spoken of by every historian of the Crusades, 'gave to his credulous neophytes such a foretaste of Paradise, that the hope of one day returning to this place of delights, made them consent to the commission of every crime, brave the most cruel tortures, and undaunted meet certain death. At a much earlier period, Sheded-ben-ad, King of Arabia, desiring to be worshipped as a God, collected in a garden, the name of which was proverbial in the East, all the delights of Paradise; and allowed them to be enjoyed by the faithful whom he deigned to admit into it. In both cases, we think that these gardens of pleasure existed only in dreams, caused among young men, habituated to a simple and austere diet, by the use of potions to which they were unaccustomed. . .' (*The Philosophy of Magic* by Eusebe Salverte, 1846).

The theory of a dream therapy, like that of homeopathic medicine, presupposes a belief in an 'astral' or invisible, but important, part of the individual physiology. Thus, if the invalid goes to sleep with the mind fortified by healing ideas, concretised in the dream state in therapeutic symbols or images, these in turn will act upon the invisible portions of the complex human organism, and assist the cure.

Where Nature has brought the work of regeneration to a halt and commands no alternative but death, dreams will explain to us, if we will heed them, the steps of the forthcoming transition and make it peaceful and edifying.

We ought not to have to make the great change save in full, happy, conscious acceptance. A better knowledge of dream technology would help eliminate the shock and fear of imminent death which at present it seems only possible to blunt by using powerful sedatives. Like dreams, the world is both enchantment and nightmare; to have known this is to have lived – and dreamed – fully. The dying have the right to the best dreams possible; a system of state medicine recognising this has yet to receive universal approbation.

A Small Glossary of
Dream Symbols & Portents,
Condensed from Several
Traditional Sources

A

Actors and Actresses. To dream of seeing performers on the stage is a lucky omen; being in their company means the reverse. Masked, they bode great danger if close to the dreamer; masked on stage, news unexpected and good.

Aircraft. Present ideas and hopes will prove fruitful.

Angels. Rather like actors and actresses, seeing them is good, trying to talk to them is not.

Animals. Dogs and other creatures symbolise the lower passions in dreams, but dreaming of them does indicate a definite progress and growing self-awareness. There is always something pleasant about a friendly cat in a dream. Horses, of all the animals, symbolise the higher or spiritual nature, of man's innate love of universal being and his capacity to attain psychic wholeness. An animal in a rage is telling the dreamer 'Beware: your passions are betraying you.'

Anchor Although this is a symbol of hope, it does not seem to be thought a good dream omen. Tradition speaks of 'news of drowning' and other dire things. The general mood or feeling of a dream, and the place of symbols in a series of dreams, should be taken into account, and so it is as well not to rush into interpreting on the basis of one symbol alone. In the Gestalt school of psychology, the analysand is asked to identify with the symbol, to try to feel its mood and purport: so often the dream symbol is part of the dreamer.

Predicted misfortunes usually seem to concern others rather than the dreamer, if that is any comfort.

Ashes. Patience will be rewarded.

Axe If the blade is away from the dreamer, it is a good time to begin new enterprises. If the blade is towards the dreamer, caution and delay will be the best course to take.

B

Baldness. Loss of friendship.

Beans. To see beans growing foretells misunderstandings. Bean flowers or their scent (and it is possible to dream of odours) herald news of a pregnancy. Dishes made with beans tell of birth or death – the latter almost certainly if dreamed of during the reign of Scorpio.

Bed. Present incapacity or ill health gives place to the birth of new ideas. If you dream you are in bed with a banker or stockbroker, good fortune is on the way through your own efforts. To dream of being in bed with a soldier means you are going to solve your difficulties with ease. . . *as* well as being attracted to soldiers. To dream of making a bed means big changes in the household. Seeing a sleeping figure on the bed means you are in love with a person and don't really want to admit it.

Begging. Begging and beggars mean slights and humiliations to come.

Blood. This dream, even if gory, typifies the life-force. The energies are to be redirected. Suppressed emotions are to have a happy outlet.

Birds. Tradition has it that if a person of wealth dreams of birds, there will soon be a serious reverse of fortune. For a poor person to dream of birds tells of coming prosperity. White birds presage sexual experience of a transitory nature. Black birds mean mourning, coloured birds social gaieties. In antiquity, dreams of quails were ill-omened.

Body (Live, human). A desire for gratification, most likely of an amorous nature, will soon be forthcoming if the opportunity is seized at the right moment. The dream embrace if the beloved, however, shows that the romance is nearly over.

Bondage. If you dream you are tied and forced to submit to your captor's will it does not necessarily mean you are a masochist but more likely lack self-confidence and need some good, down-to-earth sexual enjoyment. If the dream is the other way about, you probably need clinical help.

Box. Change your present situation and become true to yourself, or you will be stifled!

Boy. To dream of a young, unknown boy is a very lucky omen, portending great fortune and happiness.

Butter. (To eat) Quarrels with relatives.

Butterfly. Personal fulfilment, escape from danger.

Buttons. Bright buttons are lucky. Buttons chipped or tarnished foretell material losses. If the dreamer sees all the buttons dropping off his or her clothing, it means death or some other total change.

c

Candles. Four candles mean a death, three a feast, two a marriage, one a desire fulfilled – but in an unexpected manner or time, so say the old *grimoires*, or spell-books.

Castration. Beware of being enslaved by circumstances. It is time to break free!

Chains. Of iron: envious persons will try to harm you. Of gold: beware of ill-considered financial schemes. Of roses: one is coming who will bewitch your senses.

Chest (Coffer, coffin). Represents life-style and also hopes and ambitions. A dead body in a coffin means an end to misfortune and the crowning of all hopes. The dreamer's name on a coffin means that great efforts will be required to achieve what is truly desired. If an angelic hand takes the dreamer's name, written on a parchment, out of the coffin, it means that fame will come after death. To find your beloved in a coffin, or chest, whether alive or dead, means you will have your desire of him or her.

Cock crow. Every country seems to differ – some say this is a good dream, others not. Certainly, it is the herald of unusual happenings.

Cord. A knotted cord tells of an important letter to come. A long rope is a sign of sincere and helpful friendship which will be proffered the dreamer.

Crown. Of gold, fame by popular acclaim. Of silver, fame will come by underhand means or through the power of women, or that what is desired may be obtained through witchcraft. To have a crown actually put on your head in a dream is, however, unfortunate as tradition gives the meaning of 'shame and humiliation'. If the dreamer offers a crown, he or she will certainly attain pre-eminence in a certain field of endeavour.

Crystal. To see crystal glittering by the light of lamp or sun portends scandal for someone you know who heretofore has been respected.

Cucumbers. For a sick person to dream of cucumbers is an augury of returning health. For anyone else, the meaning is obviously phallic.

D

Dairy. The dairy in a dream is generally supposed to foretell a union with a plain-looking individual who will however be a good companion.

Darkness. To dream of stumbling about in the dark foretells of bad times ahead. But if you are groping towards the light, and come out into the sun and air, you will become happy again.

Dancing. Always a good dream. If dancing with someone of the same sex you will have the chance of an affair with someone of homosexual inclinations.

Death. A dream of dying means new avenues – not those beyond the grave – will soon be explored and new experiences are waiting. To dream of someone you know who has died is fortunate. However, to dream of dead people you do not know is an ill omen. To see the beloved on a deathbed means infidelity.

Debts. Some dreams take the form of demands for payment when the dreamer knows no funds are available. Similar demands, upsetting and harassing, are dreams telling us we are trying to live in a manner unsuited to our nature, and if we go on we shall meet with unhappiness and failure.

Diving into Water. Persecution, harassment.

Dolphins. If seen in a bright sea, expect an encounter with a royal person or head of state. In a dull or stormy sea – quickly change any plans recently made!

Door. Opening doors means a new chapter in the dreamer's destiny is about to begin. Opening doors, passing through rooms to other doors and continuing thus for some while means that strange lands will shortly be visited.

Dress. If a man dreams he is wearing women's clothes it may be a memory of a previous life; it may also be a fear of the responsibilities of man's estate: it might be a desire to become, or appear to become, a woman. The same is true, the other way about, if she dreams she is putting on men's clothing.

In either case, a little essay into transvestitism or getting into fancy dress might bring some glitter into the dreamer's waking life! Otherwise, dreams of clothes are held to portend the arrival of visitors from afar. Old clothes mean low vitality. A curious tradition has it that for a travelling man to dream of clothes, predicts courtship and marriage in his next stopover.

Drowning. A dream of guilt. Either the guilt must be expiated or, if it be guilt over some suppressed sexual urge, then the matter must be re-examined in a sensible way.

Drugs, Doctors (or nurses or any medical theme). Expect clear, bright eyes, a good complexion and a pink tongue for a long time to come. If you are ill, a change of treatment will produce a cure. Perhaps it is time for you to start thinking psychically, and turn to homeopathic medicine and nature cure. If you are suffering from any form of addiction, then hope is on the way: unless your addiction takes the form of pretending to be a doctor or nurse, when you should seek help – fast!

E

Eagle. Expect to soar to the heights in your own sphere of life. If very ambitious, you are going to do great things. An eagle or falcon clutching its prey, however, means speedy ruin for someone known to the dreamer.

Eggs. News of miscarriage or abortion. A broken egg tells of a virgin who will soon be ravished, not unwillingly.

Elephant. Luck. Old memories revived.

Excrement. Do not recoil! Someone is about to be very generous. This dream, which may seem disgusting, is an excellent omen. Bills will be paid, necessities obtained.

Execution. Fear of losing sexual powers, an admission of a feeling of hopelessness in the face of Destiny. Once the admission is made, it is up to the dreamer gradually to change the position in life's tragi-comedy to one of greater strength. Execution dreams may indicate that the sex life is not entirely fulfilled and that some fetish requires to be acted out: execution fantasies should be regarded with some caution, however, as with a single slip they can end in dead earnest!

Eruptions (Earthquakes, tsunami, etc). National calamities are on the way! But the dreamer will escape with his life if not much else.

F

Face. If you see your face in a glass in a dream it means your guilty secrets will soon come to light and you will be involved in scandal and disgrace.

Fair. Being in a fairground portends dismissal from employment or the winding up of a business whose failures has been caused by negligence.

Fairy. Always lucky; precious metals and jewels coming to the dreamer and perhaps a win on the pools or horses.

Fart. A dream interpreted contrarily. Embarrassment caused by farting in a distinguished assembly means that the dreamer will shortly shine in company.

Fire. A desire to commune with others on a spiritual or psychic level. Youths and maidens who dream of fire will soon know the transports of passion.

Fish. Lucky. But dreaming of trying to catch or hold a fish without success means that relationships are not going too well.

Flying, Floating. All your hopes will be realised, you will pass through every kind of difficulty and danger, and you will achieve success. Falling heavily through the air or sinking under water means you will know the sting of poverty, or, if you are rich, that you will be down to your last quarter of a million and be moaning and wringing your hands about it.

Fog. A bad dream if you are seeking help of any kind. You won't get it.

Fortress (Castle, etc). Dreaming of being locked up in such a place means you are being dominated by someone who wants more of you than you should give. If you dream you are 'king of the castle' and hold all the keys, ordering people about left, right and centre, then you may expect to make a discovery in the near future which will greatly benefit or enrich you.

Fountain. Dreams of crystal fountains are among the most beautiful and mean fulfilment and contentment. A muddy fountain, however, means base and unworthy connections, which ought to be avoided.

Flowers. Dream you are picking flowers for a bouquet and you will soon be married. If married already, then you will have a lover or mistress. If the flowers are exotic and expensive, wealth is on the way. Thorny, seedy, burry, sharp and thistly flowers means you are going to have an affair with someone you don't much care for, but which will serve your ends. Withered flowers – well, sorry, but you'd better make your will!

Fruit. Tradition ascribes good fortune to dreams of fruit, which are usually crypto-sexual. Nuts and oranges have a rather bad name in dreamland, however, and seem to be ill-omened. Yet if either oranges or nuts have pleasant associations for the dreamer, there should be no cause for dismay.

G

Games. To dream of winning a game is a splendid omen. Losing a game is not so good – beware of whoever you were playing with! You didn't recognise who it was? Brrr! Worse and worse!

Gardens. Always lucky. An untended or withered garden is a call to action.

Gems. Being covered with costly jewels in a dream is not only a reflection on your taste but shows that you are on the way down and will before long be in the gutter, and serve you right, too! (Looking at jewels, admiring them on others, is a lucky dream, however.)

Gay. (A gentleman who is attracted by other gentlemen, or a lady who finds the embraces of other ladies more agreeable than those of the heavy, boring men available.)

To dream of one who is gay, if the dreamer is not, means he or she has creative ideas of the 'castles in Spain' variety but which don't emerge in the sphere of action and achievement. Time to make the dream come true has arrived! For a gay to dream of another gay means warm, sincere friendship with a gay or non-gay, although little emphasis on sexuality.

Geese. Beware of getting tangled up with a really stupid person who may do you untold harm!

Goats. A lively time is ahead. The month of Aries will be fortunate, as will people ruled by that Star. Expect a great flow of sexual energies around you.

Gold. Gold in dreamland – expect dross on waking!

Groans. To hear groans in a dream portends the sudden disappearance in mysterious circumstances of someone you know.

Groaning Boards. To dream of being at a banquet and stuffing yourself is very unlucky indeed. To be at a banquet, or in an exotic restaurant or similar, without eating, means good things are on the way! To be in such places with beautiful, elegant and fashionable-looking people means you will end up by shunning the vain pleasures of the world.

H

Hair. A man with long hair – beware of a deceitful woman! The dreamer's hair grows long: important issues are being avoided. A

38

girl dreams her hair is falling out: she will be left, deceived, abandoned by friends and lovers. A man dreams his hair is falling out: he will become rich and successful, his sex-life will go to pieces and he will end up prosperous but bored to death and not very nice to know.

Hands. Pale, beautiful hands: spiritual help and guidance are on the way. To dream of one's own hands means one is conscious of having taken a wrong direction, but is not sure what to do next. Answer? Wait! Destiny will take charge of things! To see blood on one's hands, or on the hands of others, foretells dreadful and violent crimes. Dirty hands foretell dishonesty and abuses of confidence.

Hats. Hats giving pleasure to the wearer foretell good news about a worrying matter.

Happiness. Dreams filled with a feeling of happiness and serenity often come in a dark hour and tell the dreamer not to despair, for there are friends in Spirit, and all will be well at last.

Homecoming. Arriving at a place the dreamer feels to be home, and not entering, means that his life is yet to have some definite fulfilment and purpose. Arriving, and going in with a welcome and feeling of leaving care behind, is a presage of death. Insistent dreams of strangers arriving means that someone from the past will turn up, or that strangers will knock at the door quite soon.

Horseshoe. Good fortune awaits!

Hounds. Dreaming of hunting with hounds means you are wasting your time and not giving sufficient attention to your duties. However, if the quarry is caught, then you will succeed more by good luck than your own intelligence or application.

Husband. To dream you are happily married to a loving husband is not a good omen for your personal happiness. If you dream you have taken someone else's husband or lover, you are in some way directing your life wrongly and cannot achieve contentment as you are.

I

Ice. Ice, icicles, frozen water – don't look for success, because it won't happen! Snow, on the contrary, is a lucky dream and is a sign that all will be well in due season; bad influences will be removed and good ones will reign.

Illness. There are many 'worry' dreams and dreams of sickness are in this category. They chiefly signify that the dreamer should try to overcome anxiety and depression, and look at life more hopefully. This is often easier said than done, but at least worry dreams are a safety valve and this is especially good for those who are inclined to shut away their anxieties and try to battle on without telling anyone. A general feeling of uncertainty and perhaps too much preoccupation with the well-being of those who should be taking responsibility for their own destiny, are all productive of worry dreams. Tradition ascribes to dreams of sickness some likelihood of things going well or better for the dreamer or the loved ones. Fevers in dreams, or feeling feverish, obviously indicate a state of inner conflict.

Iron. Not fortunate in dreams as a rule. It is as well when interpreting dreams to look on the bright side. In the psychic areas the effect of optimism and pessimism are as much felt as anywhere else. It is, alas, often true that a clairvoyant endowed with a pessimistic turn of mind is more accurate than one who sees everything *en rose*, and it is often said that if you expect lovely things to happen then you will wait in vain; however, an even, balanced way of looking at things does seem to require a basically cheerful optimistic point of view. Often we do not understand why things work out as they do, with such apparent injustice; but it may be that the human entity is flung into a chaotic world in order to learn how to be strong and enduring.

Inheritance. To dream you have won or inherited a fortune means that you must expect financial troubles.

Intemperance. Dreams of inebriation, drunkards or drug fiends are very bad. They presage chaos, even if they seem to be full of gaiety.

Islands. Someone loves the dreamer, and longs for that love to be returned.

Itching. Probably some rough surface is touching the skin of the sleeper, or there may be some restlessness indicating that the sleeper's affairs are not going well, or are about to take a wrong turning. The intuition, dormant in so many of us, is often at work in sleep, transmitting warnings, through dreams, of what is to happen.

Invitations. In dreams of invitations, the symbols made use of by the intuition can be seen working in inverse or mirror fashion. The dream in this case, as with many others, is traditionally given the meaning of 'social aspirations disappointed'.

J

Jewels. Here, dream symbolism does not seem to work inversely, for dreams of jewels are always considered a good omen, while the giver of jewels to the dreamer means true friendship or love are at hand.

Jugs. To see or drink from jugs full of liquid means journeys over water. The pleasantness or otherwise of the jug's contents tells how the journey is likely to turn out.

K

Key. A bunch of keys in a dream foretells a prosperous future. A single key means a chance of change for the good should be seized.

Key and Keyhole. Desire will be fulfilled. Beware, however, of uncontrolled lust, which will bring trouble.

Kisses. Being kissed in a dream means that someone likes you but will leave you as soon as you have made it together. If you have a relationship or are married, dreams of kissing mean deception to be shortly discovered.

Knives. Freudian interpretation of dreams is often erroneous. Knife dreams are unlucky, and portend misfortune, especially through enemies.

Knots. Knotted string or rope: an important message is on the way. Knotted ribbons: an older person will take a younger partner. A ribbon with equally-spaced knots: the dreamer will soon be introduced to witchcraft.

L

Lane (Or narrow street). The dreamer is in danger of trouble with the law, or someone close to him is.

Lantern (Or any light in the darkness). You will need courage and faith in the coming time. Be steadfast!

Lark (Or any bird flying upward). Illness of a child.

Letter. If the letter be from someone you know, then news will be disappointing. If from an unknown, then good news, probably of someone you have not seen for some time.

Left Hand. A hand pointing to the left of the dreamer, or birds flying to the left (an old druidic omen, this) means that an invalid will not recover. A veiled figure standing on the dreamer's left side means an invitation to witchery and magic.

Lover. Dreams of the beloved means that the love will end due to circumstances beyond the control of either party.

An old country custom for dreaming of someone who loves you, or who will be your true love: take a piece of wedding cake baked for a virgin bride, put it in a small box bought with your own money tied up with a ribbon in which there are five knots and before going to sleep recite seven times

> Ceridwen, Ceridwen, shew to me
> The one who will my true love be.

If the wedding cake is not available, then abstain from love-making for seven days and seven nights and on the eighth day bake a small yeast or soda loaf in a new vessel, and this will do. As in all magical works and preparations it is important not to have any scratch or cut on the body and no issue of semen or menstrual blood.

Love tokens (Lovers' Knots, Pictures of the beloved, Valentines): Very unfortunate for the young. For an older person, amorous encounters with a much younger person may be expected.

Luggage. Traditionally equates with foolish, headstrong behaviour.

M

Madness. Success in any enterprise needing mental efforts, particularly examinations.

Maidens. A dream of young women or maidens is the herald of good harvests for countrymen and any pleasant thing to do with the country. For a city dweller, removal to the country. A single maid or youth in white foretells the death of such a one.

Meadows. A visit will soon be made to familiar and loved persons and places.

Migratory Birds. Take care! You may give up everything and wander off into the blue. But remember that travelling far does not necessarily mean you will learn anything more worth knowing that you can learn at home, if you have a mind to. However, if Destiny lays its hand upon you, who can prevent you from following your star?

Monsters (Dragons, sea serpents, etc.) The dreamer is beset by enemies and perfidious friends, but will escape by the skin of his teeth. A red or gold, or red-and-gold dragon foretells amazing events.

Some say that dragons in dreams symbolise self-disgust or guilt. One of the great enigmas is how far our inner states influence our exterior circumstances. Do feelings of guilt trigger perfidy in others? Does discontent within make for perfidy on the outside? The petition 'Deliver us from Evil' in the Master of Nazareth's prayer does, perhaps, mean the forces of evil on the outside, but more certainly points to the fragmented personality whose warring elements are a major cause of all ills 'of mind, body or estate'.

Moon. In a man, dreams of the moon speak of fear of the softer, more feminine side of his nature, and a need for greater inner security through self-knowledge. In a woman, the Moon in dreams warn her that she is in danger of using her power over men in the wrong way, and no good will come of it.

Murder. Dreams of murder are usually a reflection of a troubled and insecure psychic state, frustration and turmoil. However, a 'big' dream with a clearly enacted murder in it may foretell an actual tragedy.

Music. Music is sometimes clearly heard in dreams, and a hitherto unknown – or unremembered – melody may be recalled to the last note. This can happen to composers as to people who are musical philistines and have neither knowledge of nor interest in music. Why? Tradition says music in dreams is a sign of restlessness and that the dreamer will soon be packing a bag and leaving settled ways for open road or the oceans.

N

Nakedness. A sign of exhaustion, mental or physical.

Nest. Someone is going to need help. A dream of an empty nest means approaching financial difficulties for someone well known to the dreamer with disruption of the family life.

To see birds building a nest is a presage of a meeting with someone with whom the dreamer could have a lasting union.

Nightmares. These horrible experiences are the reflection of our terrors and uncertainties, or of someone else's fears and uncertainties about us. If we suffer from the torment of recurring nightmares then we have the consolation of knowing that all dreams manifest a determination in some deep, central part of our being to recognise and cope with our reality and that there is hope we shall do so – if not now, then later!

Nuns. For a girl or woman to dream of nuns, it means that her love-life is in a sorry state or soon will be. But deceptions and let-downs are the dreamer's own fault, and she must start to change her attitudes – and the type of man she chooses? For a man to dream of a nun means either that he is to be caught up in a scandal of a sordid kind, or that he is longing to 'get into drag'.

Some strange transpositions are effected in dream and fantasy, the latter being to some extent an exteriorisation of the dream. For example, a man who has been in a school run by nuns for quite a long stretch of his childhood, especially during his early adolescence, may become fixated on nuns at the same time as being ashamed of his fixation because of the inviolability of the habit; if the nuns belonged to a sternly disciplinarian order, his fixation may have a love-hate or sado-masochistic quality. Now, such a man will not dream of nuns, but will unconsciously select a substitute, and so may start to dream of, or fantasize about nurses. The streams of the imagination are often so blocked up that it is difficult to admit or even comprehend the fantasy-weaving ability of the mind. But our dreams and fantasies are as much and valid a part of our total reality as the clothes we wear or the occupations we follow.

O

Oral sex. For the voluptuary, as for the prude, this dream reflects irresolution in getting down to the nitty gritty of living. Seize opportunity with both hands instead of allowing it to slip by.

Osiris. A supernatural intervention in mortal affairs is at hand. This applies only to those who know something of the religion of Ancient Egypt. For those who do not, the dream-visitant would have to be god-like, radiant and consoling. An atheist is unlikely to have such dreams. It is difficult to know what form the dream premonition of inexplicable events would take for the out-and-out materialist; as premonitions and psychic activity do not depend upon intellectual convictions, the symbol-factories of the mind would have to make shift with, perhaps, the image of a super-bureaucrat or an outsize computer.

P

Papers (Documents). A call to action, and a need to end indecision. A paper with the dreamer's name written on it tells the dreamer not to despair but that the efforts made in life will be rewarded, not necessarily with material gain, but with fulfilment and satisfaction.

Pearls. Foretell useful connections with the highest in the land. A poor young person will see all his or her hopes realised through influential friends.

Pigeons. Pigeons flying free mean that a baby will grow up to be generally esteemed and respected. Pigeons flying round a dove-cote: an abortion.

Pigs. You are not choosing your friends with care and should change your social life. There is another interpretation which says that you will love someone who will always be true to you.

Play (Theatre). For theatrical people as well as the general public, these dreams always bode well. But theatre people should beware of dreams with clowns and masked actors in them: these portend disasters, while Harlequin and Columbine are heralds of dreadful tidings.

Policeman (Officials, Officers). If hostile or menacing, good fortune attends the dreamer, and plans will come to fruition with ease. A lone policeman, officer or official foretells the fall of a great or highly respected man; a group of them means a plot or conspiracy.

Poison. Ill-omened dreams. Prepare for misfortunes!

Posies (Bouquets of flowers). A younger person will be pursued with determination by an older, and of superior status.

Pens (Pencils). The dreamer is leaving undone something which should be attended to. This dream will probably be attended by clues as to the nature of the matter.

Post Office (Post box, Postman). Someone close to the dreamer will father a child born out of wedlock.

Potatoes. Be sure that material security is on the way. This applies to dreams of any of the staple foods.

Priest. Beware of these black ravens! Mischief is brewing!

Q

Queens. A queen speaks of ambition thwarted through the malice of others.

Quarrels. If you dream of quarrels with others, then you are not at peace with yourself.

Quicksands (Marshes). To dream of walking through ground which is unsure means that the dreamer is being bothered by temptations which are being suppressed. They should be examined in the clear light of day!

R

Rabbi. A cheerful rabbi means news of an invalid who will recover. A rabbi with a book means that the dreamer will study magical and psychic matters.

Rabbits. Not surprisingly, in view of their well-known habits, these creatures usually associate with pregnancies.

Raffles (Lotteries). Bad portents. The mind that is dwelling on gambling as a means to improve the fortunes is evidently thinking along the wrong lines. The Qabala tells us 'Accept not the word of the gambler as witness'. However, there are many reports of dreams giving winning numbers and horses which have saved the day for the dreamer; they do not appear to happen to order.

Rags and Tatters. Dreaming of being reduced to such misery that the dreamer is clad only in rags is an upside-down portent presaging good fortune, costly attire, everything expensive.

Rape. The dreamer is living in a fool's paradise, lulled by a false sense of security, and if this state continues there will be a rude awakening. If the dream is of raping another person, or seeing them raped, it is a wretched confession of the dreamer's inadequacy to face the data of life with which we have to cope from cradle to grave. What this dream is saying is 'Rise up! Face the facts! Make the best of your lot!'

Renard the Fox. There is a charming, but tricky person in the dreamer's immediate circle. Be wary of this person, but it would be a pity to lose sight of him, or her, as they have much to offer, if carefully handled, and may become much steadier with time.

Rhubarb. One of those quaint old rustic dreams which is said to foretell reconciliations.

Riding. Any kind of locomotion is a dream of progress. The more difficult the journey, the greater the progress will be. Dreams of travelling with an unknown woman are supposed to be very lucky indeed.

Ring. A broken or lost ring foretells the end of a deep relationship. Dreaming that a ring is tight and painful presages the illness of a loved one. A dream that a ring is placed on the finger is a happy one, and means that a love will be fulfilled and be lasting.

River. The dream interpreters of yore were good Freudians long before Freud. A turbulent, rushing torrent means a troubled love life and generally disturbed psyche. A smooth river with pleasant scenes on the banks means that love and daily life will go well.

s
Sailing. For a young person to dream of sailing a small boat into harbour foretells success in the chosen career.

Sailor. The dreamer will travel far and wide, and will see many strange and wonderful sights. A sailor dripping wet, as though just emerged from the sea, presages news of death by drowning at sea.

Scarecrow. Someone will offer liquor or narcotics to the dreamer.

Scissors. Another one where the goodies of the olden days anticipated Freud. For a girl, this is a dream of marriage, for an older woman, affairs and a need for discretion.

Sheep. A single sheep or a flock of them portends a happy time. But a flock of sheep scattering in different directions foretells suffering through injustice or persecution.

Sexual Intercourse. A new lover is on the way. If with a platonic friend known to the dreamer, the sex life is going to be a cause of trouble and unhappiness. Acts performed while sitting or standing mean that the dreamer is seeking higher knowledge or inspiration through sexuality. Performed in rich, palatial surroundings, the sexual act portends mental confusion and mishaps caused by the dreamer's folly or indiscretion.

Shipwreck. Tradition agrees that this is an unpropitious dream, as is any major upset on a dream journey. But seeing such upsets overtake others means that someone known to the dreamer will soon enjoy advancement and improved fortunes.

Shoes. New shoes: long journeys. Shoes which are heavy or pinch: an enterprise will not succeed. Walking barefoot: great success. Seeing shoes (or gloves) carried on a cushion means the dreamer will rise to dizzy heights.

Silver. Small silver objects or coins are unlucky, large ones the reverse.

Singing. However beautiful the singing that is heard, great sorrow is on the way, affecting both the dreamer and friends or relatives.

Snakes. There will be malicious talk about the dreamer's morals, but to dream of killing a snake foretells that the flame of a great passion will soon be fanned.

Soldiers. Heralds of change if the dreamer finds he or she has joined up and is with comrades in uniform. Destiny is about to work for the dreamer! To be in a battle, or to see brawling soldiers, means that a serious dispute is on the way for the dreamer.

Sons. Dreams of good, dutiful, affectionate sons must gladden the parent's heart. Tradition, alas, tells us that it is another 'upside down' dream and that the offspring are about to give trouble. The other way round, and all will be well.

Splendour. Folie de grandeur – delusions of grandeur – to be followed by a rude awakening.

Staircase. Ascent of stairs is thought propitious, descent the reverse. A better interpretation: a period of uncertainty will soon be resolved.

Stars. Stars clear in the heavens: good news. If they vanish before the dreamer's eyes, disappointments.

Statues. To see statues is lucky. If they move, problems will vanish like magic. But a toppling statue – watch out for danger!

Stealing. Being caught stealing is, in a conscientious person, a dream of insecurity. It follows that such a person may well be trying hard to succeed in life's battle, and by plodding along, slowly amassing credit and respect, will attain a very respectable situation – which is the traditional meaning. To dream of actually stealing something indicates a disturbed psyche, starved of affection; before love can come into the dreamer's life there must be some improvement in the quality of that life – again, the old books rightly say 'You are not making enough effort to win the regard of others and may soon find yourself lonely and in need'.

Sting. Here we are back again with the pre-Freudian Freudians. Old books say 'Maids, beware of designing men' and more candid moderns can see what is meant!

Straw. 'Straw blown in the wind', 'bricks without straw' are well-known sayings which support the meaning of this dream: an enterprise or situation has been built without enough care, and will crumble.

Sun. The way the sun appears in a dream denotes the type of omen. Clear, strong sunlight is good. A setting sun tells that something which appeared important to the dreamer is on the wane – but will in the end not be regretted.

Sword. The symbol of male power; forged from Earth's metals, dedicated to defence or attack in man's uncertain tenure of his earthly kingdom. One sword in a dream: approaching decision which will have far-reaching consequences. More than one sword: the approach of discord in home, family and love life. For those unduly unfluenced by Freud's ideas, any dream or any thought whatsoever may have a sexual significance, but only where a state of frustration or sexual unhappiness is a dominant theme in an individual's life. Protagonists of 'decency' – one of the first words to be uttered by the budding tyrant – are certain to visualise sword symbols. Nobody, however, can be coerced into virtue; good examples and a general diffusion of ideas filled with the love of goodness, truth and beauty alone can bring man to a higher state. Those who want to make every human being fit some religious or ideological mould are bound to fail, though prescriptive behaviour and repression may give the illusion of success. The marvel and mystery of the Cosmos, the infinite variety and complexity of the human entity, are veiled from the sight of canting prudes and fanatic politicos!

T

Talking. To dream someone is talking about you so that you are embarrassed is a very good dream and means your fortunes are about to improve.

Telephone. Hearing it ring – bad news. Speaking on the telephone – something helpful or useful will soon happen.

Television. Expect good news and a visit to old friends.

Thunder and Lightning. The old dream books give a number of interpretations which appear to be at variance with each other. The nearness or distance of the phenomena observed in the dream-state is accorded significance. Thunder and lightning overhead is generally held to be unlucky, further off rather lucky on the whole.

Thieves. Loss of some material possession. To suffer a theft, or to hear the old cry of 'Stop, thief' is accorded a good omen.

Tomb. A melancholy dream which nevertheless foretells the state of wedlock – whether for good or ill being by no means certain.

Torture. Being laid on the rack, or subjected to some similar form of physical cruelty, means that the dreamer is about to enjoy physical satisfactions never before experienced.

Tower. Dreaming of being in a tower, either ascending or descending, means that you are getting to grips with your reality and will shortly engage in the battle of life with energy and intelligence.

Treasure. Finding a treasure means that lean days are almost over and that fate is going to give a helping hand.

Trees. Trees being cut: danger of material loss. Trees being planted: the dreamer's memory will live long through his or her beneficent actions. Trees bearing fruit: a deserved recompense. Climbing a tree: the going is becoming heavy, and obstacles must be expected.

Trout Fishing. Generally held lucky, and portends an unexpected windfall.

Trumpets. A trumpet blast is not a good dream and should warn the dreamer of impending trouble. For the dreamer to be blowing a trumpet, surprising success is on the way.

Turnips. In every respect lucky -- portend happiness in love and the arrival of gold.

U

Ugliness. If the dream consists of the dreamer being seen as ugly or deformed, some pleasant news is coming from a far land and there will be a happy reunion with someone.

Umbrellas. If you dream of umbrellas then you may be sure it's going to rain and you won't have one – or you are putting your faith in an illusory sense of security.

Underwear. The dreamer is going to be the subject of gossip and be deserted by friends.

V

Valentines. News of death. Dreams of serenades mean the same.

Vampire. The dreamer is in a state of latent hysteria and needs peace and calm. Jasmine tea at bedtime is recommended.

Violence. The dreamer should submit gladly to the whims of the beloved. If there is no love in the dreamer's life, there soon will be, and sensual experiences hitherto undreamed-of may be expected!

Vagina. The dreamer will soon acquire a pet animal or bird. However, if the part is large and dominating, the dreamer is about to have an accident; if small and difficult to find or hard to penetrate, then the dreamer will receive many favours from a woman.

Virginity. For a young man or woman to dream that he or she loses their virginity means that there will soon be a happy marriage. However, dreams of being made love to, and then suddenly and violently forced to perform oral or anal sex, means that the young person is in danger of becoming a prostitute.

Virgin Mary. Or any Mother goddess, always fortunate, foretelling an end to woes, love for the lonely, solace to the sad.

Volcano. Someone who is in confinement or bondage will soon be free. If a passport or exit visa has been denied, it will be obtained.

Viper (See Snakes). Several of them, intertwining, means an invalid will be restored to health.

Vulture. Not an attractive bird, but lucky in a dream. If seen flying high, the dreamer's highest aspirations will be realised. If feasting on carrion, the dreamer must be content with what life offers, which will be a modest sufficiency.

W

Wading. Paddling or wading portends flirtation with a member of the same sex.

Walls. News of death which will however be a blessing in disguise.

Washing, Washerwomen. Pleasant journeys. If the laundry be patterned or flowered, a young person may expect an admirer.

Werewolf. Not usually a fortunate dream. Seems to betray a fear of strangers and may foretell an unhappy encounter.

Whips. To dream of whipping someone means that new friends are in store. But to dream of whipping an animal foretells trouble through lack of reflection. Dreams of instruments of correction without their being used is a sign that the dreamer will be able to make amends for a wrong he has done.

Wig. Wigs are dream-symbols of self-deception – and an attempt to impose on others, followed by an unmasking, or unwigging!

Windmill. Seeing a windmill, with its sails turning, means changes for the better. A windmill not in working order means that opportunities are being wasted, – a simple and self-evident kind of dream. Seeing corn being ground, or flour measured, means legal problems.

Widow. A woman who dreams she is a widow means her lover will forsake her, or her husband go off the rails. For a man to dream of a widow in black, foretells news of a suicide; if he dreams of his wife dying, he may expect to be a father or that an interest will be taken in other people's children and their welfare. A homosexual man or woman who dreams of the death of their partner may expect good fortune for both.

Will. To dream of making one's will means that many and prosperous years are ahead. But to dream of reading or hearing read the will of another means news of a death.

Wine (or spirits). Drinking either in dreamland portends dismissal, or dishonest employees, and eventual ruin.

Window. To be at a window, with people passing outside, foretells the dreamer will be in the news, and may expect to hear a deal of scurrilous talk about him. To dream of falling out of a window means a love affair or liaison which will bring the dreamer notoriety.

Wintry Landscape. Propitious: a curious traditional interpretation says that if the dreamer sees a fire or torch burning in such a landscape, then someone will throw themselves at his or her feet – but it will mean supplying their material wants.

Witch (Mage, clairvoyant, alchemist, etc). For an unbeliever, a dreadful dream, foretelling great reversals of fortune. For a believer, marvellous news is on the way.

Wolves. Beware of enemies lurking in a place you least expect.

Wool. Lucky for lovers, it is believed; the fleece on the sheep means that love will be requited: hanging on thorn bushes in shreds, a love must be wooed with perseverance: being woven, a lasting relationship will be formed. But seeing sheep being sheared of their fleece is not a lucky omen and means betrayal.

Work. To dream of being worn out by hard work means that a breakdown in health may be expected. To dream of having achieved some great work, and to be contemplating it with satisfaction is a very bad sign and means that the dreamer is wasting time and energy and that the sand in the hourglass is running away, away, away. . . . But to be hard at work, and especially at some skilled craft, means that effort will be rewarded.

Writing (or any form of communication). If the dreamer is busy writing a letter, or making a telephone call, sending a telegram, or giving a letter to a messenger, two meanings seem general: either that the dreamer may expect a business matter to come to a profitable conclusion, or that there will be a sudden, unexpected visit from an old friend.

Y
Yew Trees. Expect the passing of an aged person. If the dreamer is sitting under a yew tree, traditions state 'The days of your life are numbered', but a better interpretation is 'Your life force and psychic energies are low: you are "giving up" on life and need revitalising – otherwise indeed you may just lose the will to live.'

Yoyo (Or anything moving up and down or from side to side, e.g.

a pendulum). The fascination of both the yoyo and the pendulum lies partly in the fact that they are symbolic artefacts, representing a strong element in the human mind – its inconsistency and inclination to waver from one point of view to another. In dreams, these objects are projections of a state of mind which shows the deep concern the dreamer has to become more stable: hence the dream is fortunate, showing that by the curious combination of personal effort and the working of Fate which influence the effect of all intention, firm ground will soon be reached and a more confident approach to the future will be possible.

z
Zebra. A white person will be attracted to a black, or a black person to a white.

Zoo. Visit a zoo in the dream state and you may be sure your relations will soon be worrying you in some way. If you dream you are being exhibited in a zoo, you are on the brink of doing something shameless; if you are in such a situation and feel ashamed and terrified, you may shortly become the victim of a lecher's unwelcome attentions.

When troublesome or frightful dreams afflict us, we should raise our thoughts to our guiding spirits who will shield us from harm and bring us soothing balm for heart and mind.

Three: One Plus Nine

The form of divination set out in this chapter is an easy one, and probably as old as man's interest in such matters. Endlessly re-issued, it probably began with the casting of pebbles outside the shaman's *yurt*. The principles are those of numerology combined with what Jung called 'the principle of synchronicity' – that is, all random arrangements of objects at a given moment, if they appear to the observer to have a rhythmical manner of presenting themselves, are in some way typical of the moment *if* their message can be understood.

Some affinity with the I Ching may be remarked. The richly allusive poetic content of the Chinese oracle is absent, and the procedure more rustic and direct.

Method of Using the One Plus Nine Oracle.

Make ten lengths of noughts, each line consisting of any number set down at random and without reflection – this is important.

Example:

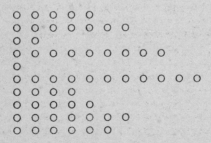

Count the number of noughts in each line, and write down whether they each come to an odd or even number. For a line adding up to an odd number, now write a single nought, and for a line adding up to an even number, write two noughts, so that ten lines of one or two noughts are obtained. From the above example, this will give:

5 noughts	=	odd number	=	O
7 ,,	=	,, ,,	=	O
2 ,,	=	even ,,	=	O O
9 ,,	=	odd ,,	=	O
1 ,,	=	,, ,,	=	O
11 ,,	=	,, ,,	=	O
4 ,,	=	even ,,	=	O O
5 ,,	=	odd ,,	=	O
7 ,,	=	odd ,,	=	O
6 ,,	=	even ,,	=	O O

Now divide the ten lines into two and place them side by side, lines 1–5 first and 6–10 next to it, thus:

A	B
O	O
O	O O
O O	O
O	O
O	O O

We now have five lines consisting of two ideograms side by side; each line of the two ideograms will contain from two to four noughts. A third ideogram has to be formed, consisting of five lines, its composition decided by whether each line of A and B yields an odd or an even number. As before, an odd number gives a single nought, an even number a pair.

A	B		C
O	O	even	O O
O	O O	odd	O
O O	O	odd	O
O	O	even	O O
O	O O	odd	O

The third ideogram (C) is the KEY. Look in the KEY CHART for the corresponding ideogram, and turn the section of the book whose Latin number is printed above it. In the appropriate section look for the double ideogram A and B as above, and note the oracle. In the given example, the oracle will be found as follows:

```
        C
    O   O
        O
        O     = XXVIII (Twenty Eight)
    O   O
        O
```

Which gives the message:

'Amorous encounters, romantic escapades, secret meetings in a discreet rendezvous.'

I	II	III	IV	V	VI	VII	VIII
IX	X	XI	XII	XIII	XIV	XV	XVI
XVII	XVIII	XIX	XX	XXI	XXII	XXIII	XXIV
XXV	XXVI	XXVII	XXVIII	XXIX	XXX	XXXI	XXXII

Ideogram No. I

Your Fate is about to change for the better. New friends and easier circumstances await you.

Entertainments, pleasure, an end to gloom are all just round the corner.

Disappointment in store – it may be business, it may be love – but it won't be too serious.

Beware of enemies and malicious tongues.

Journeys across water, changes of scene – all with good results.

If nothing is happening, just wait, change is on the way.

Don't get involved in quarrels and disputes. Avoid getting tied up with lawyers.

You will profit from boldness of decision and action.

Be careful of your safety on a journey. Danger threatens.

Someone is going to give you a good time.

A B

Unexpected news of friends or relatives far away.

Funerals, mourning.

Secret enmities and jealousy – take account of them and then go ahead and win!

You may be getting a fright. Journeys are a hazard at this time.

For a man, expect love, marriage feasts, and the enjoyment of female company.

For a woman, she will succeed in having the person she desires.

News of bereavement.

A bad time for gambling of any sort.

You will soon get what you want, with no ill effects.

Unusually good business news. Money is flying your way.

Not a good time financially. Bad news for someone in love – the end of an affair.

Stay still. Try nothing new.

For some time ahead your movements will be unsettled, and you are likely to travel.

A	B	
		All work and no play for some time to come!
		Danger of robbery or theft.
		A deception may cause you to be disappointed in someone – it's going to come out quite soon.
		Prosperity is at hand. The money or facilities you need are going to be available.
		Some news will make you sad. A final parting is near.
		News of a departure. It will be a long time before this person appears again.
		A very influential person is going to be your friend.
		Expect a difficult twelve months ahead.
		Victory over rivals, opponents or detractors.

Ideogram No. II

A B

Pack your bags! A journey is imminent.

Expect depressions. While you have them, live with them – they won't last forever.

A host of small worries and minor ailments.

A friend is going to let you down.

Stay out of trouble, or you may be in a fight.

You will hear of a fickle lover who betrays the beloved.

Health needs watching. Be careful about diet.

A sudden romantic encounter will take place.

A gift may be expected – but it will be an unexpected gift.

Be more patient. You'll get what you want – but later.

A   B

Fatal for gamblers and speculators.

Soon you will sigh with relief. Your troubles are fading.

Pluto reigns. A worrying time is ahead. Be smart and make plans for change.

Someone is going to be ill and you will have to give help.

A friend who has not been too happy is going to find their love life blooming.

For a man, expect a beautiful woman to make a play for you. For a woman, expect Lesbian overtures.

Take care. There is a thief working or living close to you.

You are deceiving yourself and telling yourself what you want to believe.

You are going to hear of a friend in trouble with the law.

The next 24 hours will in some manner be very critical for you.

Imprudence will lead you to disaster.

Visits from absent friends.

Malicious gossip is in the air.

A   B

You have adverse stars. There is nothing you can do but wait for them to go away.

The third and sixth days of next month will be very lucky. Make good use of them.

You are going to be asked to make a sudden journey.

Gold and silver will soon be plentiful.

You are to make a new friend. Fortune smiles on you.

A stormy time is ahead.

Valuables will be found, or something lost recovered.

Legacies, prizes, diplomas.

The star of your fortune is rising high.

Ideogram No. III

A	B	
		You are anxious and unfulfilled. Wait for new opportunities.
		Expect a crisis; you need not be alarmed, though.
		Your fears and suspicions are without foundation.
		A welcome sum of money is on the way.
		Problems with money.
		Serious problems with money.
		Invitations and a new circle of acquaintance.
		Annoyances from officials and persons having petty authority.
		You are surrounded by intrigue. Watch your step.
		Don't bank on your expectations. You are hoping for things which cannot happen.

A	B	
		Annoying letters and bothersome papers.
		Rivals in love and competitors in business want to oust you. They will not succeed.
		Be prudent, keep a low profile, bide your time.
		A person influenced by Saturn, probably dark and thin-faced, is a bad influence and should be avoided.
		Expect a deep-felt wish to come true.
		A profitable journey will soon be made.
		Changes of plans, probably due to unexpected visitors.
		Your vitality is at a low ebb, and things are going to appear worse than they really are.
		You are likely to be careless or neglectful of an important matter which will cause you difficulties.
		Be very careful of what you write. Some trouble with a letter or signature is to be expected.
		Do not hope for Fate to smile on you at this time. Just soldier on!
		Money is coming to you, and someone will show that they have more than an ordinary interest in you.
		You are going to be at sixes and sevens. Very good tendencies and also very worrying ones.

A B

A letter will contain things which will cause anxiety.

Lies are being spread about you. Show that you are above such things.

Someone quite unexpected will cause you trouble and anxiety.

Someone you care for is in poor health and will soon be taken ill.

A problem of a lost or mislaid letter or papers.

A sudden communication from someone not heard of for a long time.

Your luck is changing. Soon you will have good fortune.

Disappointments in love.

You are loved truly and sincerely. Look forward to a very pleasant time with some unusual good luck.

Ideogram No. IV

Your stars indicate that changes are on the way.

A long journey is likely. You will be absent from home for a considerable time.

A piece of bad luck may be expected.

Problems round the home. Watch out for fire, flood or thieves.

Be careful of what you say on the telephone or write. You are being overheard, and your letters tampered with.

Trouble with a relative.

News of civil disturbances and riots.

A sudden crisis or alarm may be expected.

You will mourn the death of someone you hold in esteem.

You are going to be involved in a scandal.

A	B	

An annoying matter, believed forgotten, will come to light again.

A bitter quarrel will leave a bad taste in your mouth.

You will emerge triumphant from a sea of troubles.

Amazing news, and a spate of great activity.

A bad omen.

Do not get involved with someone about whom you know little or nothing.

Avoid animals. You may be bitten, stung by an insect, fall off a horse, or be tossed by a bull.

An old enemy will confront and try to harm you.

Invitation to a wedding. Great rejoicings.

A happy time is in store for you!

You will receive an invitation you have coveted.

Expect some misfortune at this time.

Some very undesirable people surround you. They may do you great harm.

A B

Soon you will meet someone who will have a good effect upon your life.

You are going to lose some possession.

Do not flirt with danger, however tempting.

In the coming year you will meet three people all of whom will influence your life for the good.

If a virgin, you will soon be ravished. If not, someone will have their way with you.

Go ahead with your plans, in spite of misgivings.

You are in danger of giving great offence to someone influential.

It is a bad time to begin anything new. Wait for better conditions.

You are an old worryboots. Stop it! Life is much brighter than you believe.

Ideogram No. V

A   B

You are going to cross a great ocean.

You are going to be busy with papers, manuscripts and documents – all good for you.

News of the death of an enemy. Your life will be more peaceful because of it.

You have just lost an opportunity and you ought to be kicking yourself.

Good for gambling and speculation.

You are going to buy something very cheap, or someone will do you a good turn.

Victory! However heavy the odds, you will win!

Great rejoicings are on the way, and you will take part.

Nothing is going well at this time, so don't expect much cooperation or satisfaction from anyone.

You should set to work to overthrow your enemies, and you will succeed.

A B

Breakers ahead! Retreat rather than advance.

Messengers of unexpected tidings.

Sad news is coming.

The Angel of Death is near: you, however, will be spared.

Good luck, prosperity, a really fortunate time.

You are going to meet someone you know who has been or soon will be broken by misfortune.

Insecurity reigns round you. There will be money losses and perhaps a robbery.

Your enemies are out to get you, so be warned and outwit them.

Within a year you will be united with a tall, fair man.

Very good luck – but do not make any speculative decisions on a new moon, or during a lunar eclipse.

A professionally attractive young woman, perhaps an artiste or model, will become your friend.

Conflict and trouble in work and home.

The force of evil is a very real one: it approaches you, so summon up all that is good, strong and brave.

71

A   B

You are in danger of being arrested, or at least subjected to an unpleasant inquisition.

You are trying for the wrong objectives. Take a new look at things – and at yourself.

Protect your house. See yourself well guarded. Go into lonely places with lights and weapons.

If you have lately had setbacks, take courage – Fate is going to do you a very good turn.

Someone is going to try to cheat you. You will have to make a journey. You will meet a charming individual.

You are going to be tempted by vicious persons to join their debaucheries.

Take care of your health. You are inclined to neglect it and this may lead to trouble in the near future.

A happy time, parties, pleasure and good company.

Conflicts will have to be resolved, squabbles over material things to be settled. Some losses likely.

Ideogram No. VI

A B

Be careful of 'fair words and false promises'

Go ahead! Don't worry! The way is clear.

Good things to do with money are on the way.

You are approaching a new cycle of uninterrupted good fortune.

Unexpected journeys and happenings.

You are off on an adventure involving travel, and with good companions.

Someone is in trouble, and you will hear about it sooner or later.

There will be an empty seat round the family table before long.

Books and papers are going to keep you busy and you will find something of interest among them.

Sudden and surprising news is on the way.

A **B**

You are soon going to be changing your address.

Generally favourable. Expect a sum of money to come unexpectedly.

Some sad events are going to occupy your mind.

Take care of your health. Your vitality is not too good, so don't be surprised if you feel low.

Expect good fortune with precious metals, stones, or objects of value.

A secret is about to be revealed.

A dark star approaches: sickness and accident are in the air.

A bad portent: do not expect things to go well. Put off decisions.

A removal – perhaps someone close to you, perhaps your own.

Confusion, uncertainty, lost papers or addresses.

Not a lucky month ahead. Nothing goes really well, so just lie low till the moon changes again.

Beware of intriguers and mischief-makers.

Within a year you will be a mourner at a funeral!.

A	B	
		The pleasures you think you enjoy are going to turn to dust and ashes.
		Splendid gifts are on the way to you.
		Grasp a wonderful opportunity which will soon come your way: don't pass it by.
		You will hear of troubles affecting important people, which will also affect yourself.
		Take care not to give offence to someone who will bear you a grudge.
		However gloomy the outlook, things are going to be really good for you.
		You will have to make elaborate preparations for a journey.
		News of accident or illness which will give you sorrow.
		You are moving in the direction of disaster – draw back before it is too late.

Ideogram No. VII

You are going to be cheated over a money matter.

News of a traveller.

Grief and sadness are in the air.

Sudden death due to a calamity.

Aches and pains and fever are on the way.

Illness due to worry and pressure.

Someone thinks they are about to triumph over your downfall: they are very wrong and you will win.

Indiscreet things are going to be said and cause trouble.

If you are rather reserved and retiring you are about to come out of your shell.

A brief time of great, hectic enjoyment, followed by a reckoning.

A B

Ill omened.

A time when you make enemies without meaning to do so.

You seem to be getting deeper into anxieties without much constructive thought to relieve yourself of them.

Unexpected news by post or in the newspapers.

You are waiting to hear the outcome of an important matter. Soon you will be joyful.

Treachery: your position is being undermined.

Disappointments concerning friends and journeys.

Ill omened.

After a quiet time, everything is going to happen at once.

You are going to meet a sailor or someone who has been travelling around for a long time.

You are being lulled by a false sense of security. All round you there are traitors and spies.

A false and designing woman is doing harm to you and your friends.

Very good luck indeed. A really golden omen.

A B

Good fortune, especially through letters, cables or telephone.

Friends are going to be dividing into factions and quarrelling among themselves.

You are to have a very restful time, lying around and doing nothing.

A beginning to a project looks promising – but it will come to nothing.

Invitations from the rich and famous.

Things are now to happen which can form a solid base for future prosperity.

Disappointments – they are written in the stars.

Troubling career or business news.

Expect a lively time and you will feel on top of the world.

Ideogram No. VIII

A heavy responsibility faces you, and it is your duty to see it through.

News of people leaving their own country to settle in a new one.

A wish almost impossible of realisation – an objective seeming beyond reach – keep on, and success will come at last.

You will hear of a suicide.

An uproarious celebration is on the way.

You have made a true and lasting friend.

Rage, and anger – cruel words and blows.

Something you hope for is not going to happen.

Surprising bargain or profit, through something quite unexpected.

A legacy or, as an old book says 'Gain by the dead'.

A   B

Someone is going to bite the hand that feeds them.

Duplicity and intrigue surrounds you.

Reconciliations and good news. Gain. Good news.

Do not hold back from cheerful company which will do you good.

Fate is going to achieve something for you with no effort on your part.

Take care of what you put your name to: there is great danger over a signature or agreement.

Solid material satisfaction is on the way.

Interesting and even brilliant people are going to demand your presence.

This is a time for romantic dalliance and sexual conquest.

Someone loves you, and you will hear from them.

Fate will see to it that you thread your way through a maze of difficulties.

You will be asked to make a journey, suddenly and urgently.

At present it is not a lucky time for you. All travels and movement benefit you, however.

80

A   B

Persevere: you are not lucky at present, but wait – the darkest hour is before dawn!

The way is clear. You will now advance easily. You are going to find a key to great riches or renown.

Expect disappointments and that nothing will go as you plan.

Conditions of general insecurity prevail round you. Be very cautious.

An important letter or message is on the way. It may be an unpleasant surprise!

Expect some very interesting developments in your life within one week.

Indications of an unpleasant misunderstanding with someone, especially if you do not guard your tongue.

Irritability, liverishness, and a dark view of things do not assist you in making decisions just now.

You are going to have to be on your guard against a redheaded man or woman.

Ideogram No. IX

An influential person will soon do something helpful for you.

Money or valuable gifts are coming from over the sea.

An unexpected gift is on the way. It will be something artistic and beautiful.

A friend will soon be met who can be counted upon to act with kindness and generosity.

If money is needed for a special purpose, it is coming. Friends are going to rally round and support you.

However little you may expect it, if you are single you will be wed within a year.

Don't be broken-hearted if your present ventures fail. Destiny has other things in store.

Dangerous journeys. Deceitful women. Damaging letters and sinister documents.

Flee from lawyers and lawsuits – they will bring only trouble. Do not expect justice.

The Angel of Death is at hand, and will visit one you know well.

A   B

Plotters are seeking to secure your downfall. Caution and retreat should be your policy.

You will wipe out your enemies in a great victory.

You are to be visited by a phantom from your past.

Loss of material things.

News of an accident by one of the four elements — earth, air, fire or water.

Weeping and wailing will soon fill the air about you.

Do not give in to persuasion or coercion.

Beware of bandits if you are travelling, and of robbers if you are at home.

Words spoken in haste may cause an irreparable breach.

You may be unable to avoid a lawsuit, but try to get an opponent to see reason.

You are going to be restless: far horizons are beckoning.

Sad news will make you want to change many aspects of your life.

An irresponsible person is going to cause great damage or mischief.

A	B	
		Nothing goes harmoniously. Fate may be telling you to seek change.
		If things are uncertain, firm decisions and action are soon going to put things to rights. The moment for these things to happen is near.
		Happy friends will invite you to share their joy.
		A bad omen.
		A very bad omen.
		Within a month, expect changes in your life for the better.
		Big changes, long journeys, new horizons.
		A woman is going to become pregnant and a scandal will result.
		Prepare for sudden dismissal and exile from familiar surroundings.

Ideogram No. X

A   **B**

You are going to get involved in other people's troubles.

News of death in a far-off place.

Maybe this will be very good, maybe just fair . . . try and see.

A long journey is in sight.

Money is coming to you.

Someone of higher standing than yourself will bestow something of value upon you.

In three weeks you will make a new friend.

You will take part in a festival.

A very busy time ahead. You will make decisions important to others.

A woman is going to give you cause for anxiety.

A   B

A bad omen.

News of illness or accident.

You will come out of dangers and difficulties unscathed.

You will have to change your plans because of a project's failure.

Heights and depths, joys and sorrows intertwine, but your fortunes remain set fair.

After a serious setback, the sun will come out.

A wedding is being prepared.

Assemblies and conferences where you will make a good impression.

Bickering and misunderstandings. Be diplomatic.

A time of sorrow over death is near.

There are breakers ahead. Steer carefully.

Be very cautious. Make no move rather than a false one.

Money troubles.

A B

Changes of plans, muddles over arrangements.

This will be a very lucky time for you.

For a woman, a declaration of passion. For a man, emotional storms.

Everything you are now planning will go ahead smoothly.

Property and money are going to cause disputes.

Stop worrying about the ways and means of getting what you want. They will appear out of the blue.

Expect the unexpected with the next twenty-four hours.

A sign of fatigue. You need rest and time for thought.

You are going to have the opportunity of moving house.

Ideogram No. XI

A   B

A full moon will see big changes for you.

A long voyage over the sea may be expected.

Don't try to get anything completed at this time.

Petty troubles and anxieties. Keep a balanced view of things and try to have a sense of humour.

A time will be spent in the company of someone who will give you sensual delights scarcely dreamed of.

Someone is telling you lies and misinforming you.

You are about to enter the halls of the mighty.

Your dearest wish is to be fulfilled.

After struggling for a definite objective, you will obtain it in spite of earlier defeats.

Great honours are in store for you. You will be in a position of authority.

A   B

Not too happy a time in the next seven days.

You have to go out and get what you want – just hoping for it won't achieve anything.

Much movement is indicated, and nothing much settled by it.

A very important investment will be made, probably in house property.

Wedding plans will be put off.

Relax, enjoy yourself – everything conspires to make things pleasant.

A curious relationship will give rise to mixed feelings.

You are making enemies, which is the last thing you ought to be doing.

Restoration of health for an invalid, and a secure financial position.

You are going to do something deserving of a reward, and will be pleasantly surprised.

If you are rich and haughty, prepare to be brought down to the dust. If you are poor, prepare for a great surprise.

Eros is not your friend at this time: love affairs do not prosper.

A prisoner will be released. Someone in trouble will be made happy. But an invalid will die.

89

A B

Beware of over-indulgence: it will harm you seriously.

Soon you will be putting on new clothes and making your home beautiful.

A very lucky omen.

Good luck, unless this oracle is cast on a new moon, when the reverse is the case.

Now everything will go more easily for you, and the remainder of your life will be long and contented.

You are in danger of ruin through deceit and lies.

A quarrel which could be dangerous should be avoided.

A very bad omen. Take great care of what you say and do and all will be well – but only just!

Sickness among children or animals.

Ideogram No. XII

A **B**

A very young bride or bridegroom will give rise to much talk. An old person is going to have a new lease of life either by marriage or late success.

A good journey and safe return.

You are living in a dream. Soon you will have a rude awakening.

Beware of dishonest employees or employers.

In old age you will be covered with honours and wealth. The great will flock to see you.

Patience! You will know much better times.

Unexpected gain – but it is a question of easy come, easy go!

Jewels, valuable coins, or rich ornaments will be yours.

You will be unexpectedly remembered in a will.

Through folly you are going to ruin all you have gained. But you will learn your lesson and build again.

A B

Impeachments, arrests, and plots in high places.

You are doing something you should not. Beware, for it will become a subject of scandal.

A feast, followed by mourning.

You are going to meet someone both reliable and sincere. They will be a great help to you.

Be on your guard, as you are in danger of having all you possess taken from you.

Swift journeys by land or air, with little time for preparation.

Removals and journeys are ahead, but they mean problems for you.

Next Saturday is an ominous day. Stay indoors and do nothing.

You will triumph over a wicked person.

Very good omen.

Girls! If you think you've met 'Mr. Right', take care – you are going to get hurt.

A relative may meet with a nasty accident.

A coveted invitation is coming. You will have to look your very best and make a good impression.

A   B

If you are buying lottery tickets or are doing the pools, you are going to be lucky.

You are going to arrange or negotiate some matter with great success, and be rewarded.

A dangerous omen presaging falls, knocks, and wounds from animals or wild things.

News of people you have not seen for a long time.

Someone is going to be taken suddenly ill.

You are going on a long and arduous journey

A messenger will tell you something surprising.

You are going to have money worries for some while.

On no account move house or change your job.

Ideogram No. XIII

You are in danger of being robbed in a holdup, or kidnapped. Keep your wits about you.

A fair-haired man or woman is going to do something which will be to your advantage.

Someone is on a long journey and is approaching your house. Romance is in the air.

A letter will bring money, or news of it.

For the next year you are going to be very lucky.

If you are in business, now is the time to expand. Your work will be well rewarded.

A competitor will try to discredit you.

You are going to hear bad news.

Employees are bad news. They are going to cause a lot of trouble.

You are being talked about with spite. Watch your name is not being used without your authority.

A   **B**

You are easily deceived and are going to be made to look foolish by a person of ill will.

Men! Watch out for a designing woman. She is a threat to your well-being and peace of mind.

You are going through a difficult time. It is almost over and your stars will soon be better.

If you are looking for money you will get it. If you need new business, it is on the way.

Within six months you will change your address.

You lack caution. Look before you leap.

Travels, changes of address, all beneficial.

Weeping and wailing for an untimely death.

For a woman, you are to meet a seducer. For a man, a woman is out to get you and not let you go.

Within a week, your hopes will be crowned in an unusual manner.

Losses in business. On no account take risks. Make no generous gestures.

Remember, no good deed goes unpunished.

If you are worried about making no progress, your stars will change in about six weeks.

A   B

If you have a friend who is far from home, and needs warning about something, get in touch quickly.

The death of an enemy is at hand. A great deal of money is somewhere about, and you will get some of it.

A poor omen. Things look pretty mediocre.

News of an excellent marriage, firmly based on good prospects.

Danger of loss of money and illness. You will help prevent it.

You must expect a month of troubles.

Someone is persecuting you. You are going to be harassed. Nothing comes easily at this time.

Your health is not good, and you have no pleasure in love.

A new friend will be shy at first, but later you will know him/her better, and be happy with the friend.

Ideogram No. XIV

You have problems which are not easy to solve at present. Try not to get too depressed.

News of friends in difficulties.

Either a move or great change in your present home.

Anxieties, but passing ones.

A good omen.

A rather cheerless time will be ended by good news about cash.

If you have cast this oracle on a Sunday or feast day, you will be wealthy later in your life.

News of death, someone who is known to you but not a friend.

Someone you would dearly like to see again will soon be with you.

Don't expect things to go well for the rest of this year.

A B

Someone is trying to take advantage of your good will. Don't be a sucker.

If you imagine that someone you know doesn't like you, think again. Your coolness to each other may give rise to different feelings.

Good luck is in store for you. Make a decision and it will turn out well.

A very lucky journey is ahead. You will return better off than you went.

For a woman, expect to be courted by an ardent admirer. For a man, a male friend thinks of you with deep affection.

For a woman, beware of a red-haired seducer. For a man, beware of someone with red hair who is insincere.

A supposed friend is saying unkind things about you. You will find out and confront the viper.

If you have a known enemy, beware of any kind gesture on his or her part. On no account accept anything from them or go anywhere with them.

Low vitality will affect your efficiency. Things soon will improve.

Sad news from far away.

Good news in a letter. Anything to do with the written word will prove very lucky for you.

You must persevere. There is a tendency to give up too easily – and things will eventually turn out well.

Business letters or documents contain a hidden sting.

98

A B

You are going to have a lucky escape from danger, within the next week or so.

Good news for those in love. Profit and a good stroke of business concluded.

If you are connected with civic affairs or social work, then you have very good news on the way.

You are going to be in the thick of troubles, but they will not affect you.

Take care of fine words and false promises. You are deceiving yourself about someone's sincerity.

It is dangerous for you to cross water for the next two months.

Unexpected good fortune is going to surprise you and maybe cause a change in your plans.

Say farewell to one you love – a final parting is near.

You must visit a doctor if you are not feeling well.

Ideogram No. XV

A   **B**

Well-formed plans are going to succeed beyond your wildest hopes. You can soon be relaxed and happy.

Good news for Cinderellas. The golden coach and Prince Charming are coming.

You are soon going to travel, and it will have a very good result.

It is time for you to be up and doing. Make decisions, make changes!

A bad time to start anything new. Wait till the conditions are just right.

One who says 'I love you' also loves others.

You are going to enter into a struggle from which you will emerge victorious.

Don't make plans as you are going to have to take time off unexpectedly.

Surprising news of someone whose memory has almost faded.

Excellent for business. Deals in gold and precious things will succeed beyond expectation.

A   **B**

Have nothing to do with a possible lawsuit. It will turn out badly for you.

Your wish will soon come true.

Some luck is on the way, but keep what you have with care, as there is a danger of losing it.

A nice surprise may be expected.

You are going to be badly advised about an important matter by someone who appears to be trustworthy.

News of ill health, pain and suffering.

You are about to have a really wonderful time.

For young people, love and joy. For old people, peace and contentment.

Someone is attracted to you, and will soon declare themselves.

You are in danger of offending someone of importance.

You are going to overcome all antagonisms and rivalries.

You are in danger of being ruined by scandal.

Within a month your health is going to suffer in some way.

A   B

Someone poor and lonely is in need of help.

Try to see that someone you know is in need of comfort – you can do something for them, and should.

If you are worried about changes, everything is going to go smoothly.

Feeling down, poor, neglected? Soon everyone will be courting you!

Good news in the mail, and a pleasant surprise over money.

You have adverse stars. Wait for them to change.

Cast on the 4th, 5th or 20th of the month, expect news of a funeral. Otherwise, news of someone in trouble who makes a good recovery.

You are going to quarrel with a loved one. Cool it.

One of your best friends is about to be involved in a very unpleasant business.

Ideogram No. XVI

If you are hoping for good news, it will be the opposite.

Don't travel. You will be in trouble if you do.

If you are feeling on the up and up, beware: it is now a time of testing when you require caution.

If you are putting a lot of effort into something and not succeeding, stop worrying and start something new.

What a lucky time for you! You can have all you desire within reason before many weeks are past.

People who may have been cool to you are now going to change their minds and open their doors to you.

You have enemies, although you have done nothing to deserve them. They are trying to harm you.

A bad omen.

A business man can expect reverses which will plunge his family into misery. A lover is going to be badly hurt.

Be careful of catching viruses and other infections.

A B

Don't expect the weather to be on your side.

Do what you can, hope for the best, and things will turn out more or less well.

Cast the oracle on a new moon and you will have a long and surprising journey. Other days, love troubles.

You are surrounded by difficulties and nobody is being helpful, but you will win through.

You are going to travel, and will do well from your journey.

Prepare to shed tears, perhaps of mortification.

Invitations, gifts, parties.

Really wonderful stars are about to bless you in the best possible way.

Those who think they love you are trying their best – and doing their worst for you.

Expect a stab in the back.

You are going to have to work hard to get what you want, so set to!

Trade is going to be spectacular.

A reunion with an old friend, a visit to a beloved place.

A	B	
⊙ ⊙⊙ ⊙⊙	⊙ ⊙⊙ ⊙⊙	News of wars, revolutions, epidemics and famines which may affect you adversely, but not fatally.
⊙ ⊙⊙ ⊙⊙	⊙ ⊙⊙ ⊙ ⊙	Don't believe a word you are told by someone who makes grand promises, or tries to get you to do something for hope of a great reward.
⊙ ⊙ ⊙ ⊙ ⊙	⊙ ⊙⊙ ⊙ ⊙	Troubles in love!
⊙ ⊙ ⊙ ⊙ ⊙ ⊙	⊙ ⊙ ⊙ ⊙ ⊙	Your love or marriage partner is about to make life miserable for a while. Business associates will give you a hard time.
⊙ ⊙ ⊙ ⊙ ⊙ ⊙	⊙ ⊙ ⊙ ⊙ ⊙ ⊙	Valuables and possessions are in danger of damage or loss.
⊙ ⊙ ⊙ ⊙ ⊙ ⊙	⊙ ⊙ ⊙ ⊙ ⊙	Soon you will be in easier circumstances: but remember to give to charity or you will lose what you have gained.
⊙ ⊙ ⊙⊙ ⊙	⊙ ⊙ ⊙⊙ ⊙	Before a week is past, you will hear news you are waiting for.
⊙ ⊙ ⊙ ⊙ ⊙	⊙ ⊙ ⊙ ⊙ ⊙	You are going to have to learn a new language or take up a new craft.
⊙ ⊙ ⊙ ⊙ ⊙ ⊙	⊙ ⊙ ⊙ ⊙ ⊙ ⊙	Death by sea or air.

Ideogram No. XVII

A   **B**

Go ahead with your plans. They will succeed and your general situation will improve greatly.

Cast this oracle on a Saturday and you will do well to make no plans or decisions today or tomorrow.

You need change of scene and will get it.

Nothing is settled, so don't try to put things on a permanent basis at present.

Cast on the 5th, 8th or 12th day of the moon, sad news: otherwise a number of small monetary gains.

Get busy! You can be successful with any project involving finance.

You are in no frame of mind to do anything important. Delaying tactics are best. Relax: rest is needed.

Sickness is in the air. Avoid infections.

There is a spice of danger in what you are doing. You may have to go ahead, but do so cautiously.

Your hopes and expectations are fraught with dangers.

A B

This is a bad oracle for the love life.

Somehow you are going to get from A to B even if you have to walk all the way.

Don't take refuge in optimism. Prepare for the worst possible outcome.

You are going to be betrayed in a cruel manner.

Sudden news of absent friends.

A change of plans is coming.

Good luck, wishes fulfilled, wedding bells.

Your house is blessed. Contentment will blossom beneath your roof.

An impulsive word may make you an enemy. Guard your speech.

You are going to set out on a journey.

Steer clear of the countryside. It bodes you no good. Stay in town!

Don't try to get friendly with someone who acts rather distant: they will misinterpret everything.

If you need furniture, objects, consumer goods – they are on the way.

A	B	
		Do not get involved in a law suit or similar complications.
		You will see your hopes realised in the end, so persevere.
		A good time for any kind of business or making a quick profit.
		During this month you may have accidents, and try most especially to avoid going near deep water.
		Invitations. You are going to be much talked about in a nice way.
		A wonderful omen.
		The law is likely to be making some enquiries. You may have troubles from unscrupulous persons.
		You may be involved in a scandal if you don't take care.
		Good forces are on your side. All will be well.

Ideogram No. XVIII

A **B**

Do not hope for mercy. Your enemies will not spare you. A dreadful omen.

Death of a friendship.

Sad news about people you know and whose interests you have at heart.

Don't move house or business premises. You will regret it. If you have to move – consider it temporary.

Your projects cannot succeed.

There are very dark influences about you. Evil may seem to be triumphing. Patience! Pray!

A great deal of talk and nothing achieved.

A troubled time is ahead, with heavy burdens.

If cast on the 9th day of the moon: Frauds and impostures. At other times: you are not doing your best.

Something very unusual is about to take place. If not agreeable, it will at least be extraordinary.

A   B

For a woman: proposal of marriage. For a man: you are loved by one you do not love.

The family scene is bad. No joy or pleasure there!

An old man or woman is going to be your friend and benefactor.

You are surrounded by second-rate, Mickey Mouse people: get away from them.

If you are covering yourself with furs and jewels now, in a few months you will be stripped bare.

A fatal cause of extravagance is near you.

You are in poor shape and your work and image are suffering. Do something about it before it is too late.

You are being misinformed and slandered.

If you have troubles now, don't worry, your old age will be serene and secure.

Love, travel, the arts and sciences, all bring good to you.

Fate is about to shower good fortune upon you.

A beautiful woman is going to cause a lot of trouble.

You are not treating someone well and it is a cause of difficulty for you if you don't take care.

110

A	B	
○ ○ ○ ○ ○ ○	○ ○ ○ ○ ○	Beware of the four elements – earth, air, fire and water.
○ ○ ○ ○ ○	○ ○ ○ ○ ○	Your hopes and expectations are about to receive a great blow.
○ ○ ○ ○ ○ ○	○ ○ ○ ○ ○	Secret meetings and seduction are in the air.
○ ○ ○ ○ ○	○ ○ ○ ○ ○	A difficult encounter will finish in delight.
○ ○ ○ ○ ○	○ ○ ○ ○ ○	There is sickness near to where you live. You may hear of the sudden death of a neighbour.
○ ○ ○ ○ ○ ○	○ ○ ○ ○	A dangerous time for the health.
○ ○ ○ ○ ○ ○	○ ○ ○ ○ ○	Take out an insurance policy. You are going to need it.
○ ○ ○ ○ ○ ○	○ ○ ○ ○ ○	There is going to be conflict over a will or the property of someone who has just died.
○ ○ ○ ○ ○ ○	○ ○ ○ ○ ○ ○	You are living in a fool's paradise and handling false gold.

Ideogram No. XIX

A B

A priest or man or woman of God is about to enter your life.

A lot of money will surround you: some of it may rub off on you.

You will soon find yourself sitting with someone of the highest rank. You will become prosperous soon after.

An old flame is about to be seen again, with some emotion.

Remember that 'a verbal agreement isn't worth the paper it's written on'. A real snake is trying to harm your interests.

A troublesome, mean, spiteful person is hard to avoid, but should eventually be cut out of your life.

A very good omen.

A messenger of glad tidings is on the way.

Excesses may prove dangerous or even fatal. Curb your appetites.

The desired person will soon be yours and melt beneath your kisses.

A   B

If someone gets aggressive, turn and run.

You are going to have a lucky escape.

A light fingered person is around. Lock up the trinkets!

A good omen. You are going to have good news.

A great shame is about to come upon your house.

You may become distraught with anxiety, as things will go badly for some time. Try to be hopeful.

After being an object of scorn and contempt, you will rise to great heights.

Someone you hate is going to meet a bad end.

Letters and parcels will bring excellent news.

You are being unsure in your judgements, over-nervous and unconfident.

Someone who has been worrying you will leave your orbit. Expect a very strange visitor.

Not a good omen, especially where money is concerned.

Cast on a Friday this means important news: on a Sunday, money: on a Monday, a journey within a week: Tuesday: quarrels: other days – disagreements on matters of mutual concern.

113

A   **B**

Cast on Thursday or Sunday: money coming: on the 12th day of the moon: legacies.

Hard work will be rewarded, so don't get discouraged.

A friend will soon be coming.

There is a lot of talk about doing things, but not much action: get things moving or there will be no results.

Much heaviness and responsibility. You may stagger under your burdens, but it won't be for very long.

Your ambitions are being thwarted by malice.

Beware of contagion and infections.

Bad news. Cast on a Monday, expect the worst.

Your projects seem to bring hard work and no rewards.

Ideogram No. XX

A B

Don't worry if Destiny has withheld her favours – you are soon to be the spoiled darling of Fate!

Money is coming – a great sum which will secure your situation.

New opportunities in business are going to demand quick thinking and changes.

You are wasting your life in idleness and fantasies.

The dark clouds in your life will soon vanish.

A friend is arriving who will give you much to think of.

If you desire someone, you will have your way with them.

A very good omen.

Letters will tell you something important but good: you may rely upon the information they contain.

Three times within a year you will make a momentous journey.

A B

You are surrounded by slander and deceit.

Joy will be changed to sorrow, plans will be cancelled, hopes dashed.

Someone is trying to do you harm, and there are spies about.

A very bad omen. Legal matters end in ruin or jail.

Do not speculate or gamble. Cling to what you have.

You may expect a bad time financially, then there will be a remarkable change for the good.

Storm clouds are going to disappear, and there is someone who wants to make you happy.

You will now be able to do something you have not been able to do.

Danger of accident in sport or hunting.

A dear one will go into Spirit within a twelve-month.

Do not lightheartedly take on a burden which would become insupportable.

A person dear to you will be buried in a foreign land.

Someone outwardly attractive is cunning and dishonest.

A   B

A time of ups and downs, running about, and removals.

Some people not very friendly to you are clanning together and will be an obstacle in your path.

Be careful. This is not a good time – your stars are unfavourable.

A very good omen. Cast on a Thursday, expect great joy.

You are being inconsistent, uncertain of yourself and a burden to others. Snap out of it.

Misunderstandings over small matters. Embarrassments.

Cast on a Saturday: hope and help are near. Other days: stay indoors if you can, otherwise take care of yourself.

You may expect a win or a prize.

Your good angel is going to be very helpful.

Ideogram No. XXI

A B

Pay attention to your dreams. They will tell you something you should know.

Beware of water.

You or someone you care about is going to lose money.

A lucky omen.

You are going to pay dearly for a pleasure which you will regret.

Take care of spells and witchcraft. Wear a powerful talisman.

Bad advice, masking as good, will cause you great difficulties if you are not vigilant.

Food and drink may contain poison or be unwholesome.

Prepare for a time of intense activity.

Not an easy time ahead. Don't expect triumphs.

A **B**

Your hopes are not at present going to be realised.

A disaster will befall a friend very soon.

Money and sexual pleasure are yours for the asking.

A quarrel with a woman will end in kisses.

A false lover will cause great unhappiness to a tender soul.

A bad omen, indicating financial insolvency and physical exhaustion.

You are going to meet someone who will become a true friend.

It would be profitable for you to emigrate and start a new life in another land.

News of someone you thought long dead.

Beware of drugs and narcotics and those who use them.

A merciless creditor will try to ruin you.

You are going to be staring disaster in the face – and will escape by a miracle.

Money is coming for a special purpose.

A   B

Expect a happy time. Put care aside and enjoy it.

Losses will be made up by a generous action. But someone in trouble may try to end their woes.

Beware of a man or woman who preys on others.

Cast on Monday or Wednesday: annoyances will cloud your sky this week. Other days: expect the unexpected.

Two people will part. One will come towards you.

Danger from wickedness masked in luxury and gold.

Animals and vehicles are a danger this next day or so.

You are going to suffer heavy material loss.

A young man or woman, now poor and despised, will become rich and famous. Be their friend!

Ideogram No. XXII

A **B**

Seven years of good fortune are ahead. Use your opportunities, for there is also a temptation to be idle.

A wealthy person far away will remember you in their will.

Do not imagine that someone is interested in you – you are deluding yourself.

Journeys are useful, if they have a definite object. Mere wandering and idling will bring you home in a bad state.

There is money coming to you.

Brilliant good fortune is coming your way.

Invitations to parties and rejoicings.

A relation will be married soon, or re-married. You may expect to be fortunate at this time.

Bad news about people you know will cause talk and you may have to change your plans.

A woman and her lover are your enemies.

A B

A tissue of lies and falsehood will soon come to light.

An employee or servant is going to rob you.

You are making a comfortless bed and will have to lie upon it.

A very good omen.

There is treachery at hand. You should strike first.

Fate is going to set you on the right path by a curious trick of fortune, which may be somewhat disagreeable.

Dreadful news about people you know and respect.

You are innocent, but this will not prevent your being judged with cruel unfairness.

An ardent lover will be transformed into an excellent spouse.

Danger from contamination or poison.

Publicity is bad for you just now. Lie low.

Your way of life is doing you harm. You need change.

You will see your ambitions fulfilled, your pride will know no measure, your fortune will be immense: but there will be a terrible bitterness in your cup of joy.

A   B

Priests, men or women or God, are drawing near to you.

You are living on vain hopes.

A bad omen – one of the worst in this Oracle.

Escape from sudden danger will be sure, even at the last moment.

Anger will be followed by smiles, a loss by a gain.

You are in danger of being charmed by a person or situation which can do you great damage.

You are in danger of accident.

You are soon in the midst of intrigues. You will destroy your opponents.

Your life will be longer than anyone you know.

Ideogram No. XXIII

A	B	
		Misfortune; you will be blamed and castigated, and, if employed, dismissed.
		A bad omen. Unhappiness over the house and place of work.
		Painful, difficult journeys. A time of great change.
		A friend or lover is coming to stay with you.
		You are going to be surrounded by wealth, and you will certainly get a little of it.
		Scandals and grief over money.
		A person with an open, honest face is a sink of iniquity and seeks to harm you.
		A bad time for money matters.
		Unexpected and dramatic news.
		A very sociable time ahead with valuable introductions.

A   B

You are going to be disappointed – and justly so.

A bad omen, foretelling accidents. and news of them.

Do not travel. Your presence is needed at home.

Girls! A wonderful man is going to fall for you, but you will have to do exactly what he wants or he will quickly tire of you. Men – expect a rival.

You are to be mixed up with mean, low people.

Annoying news. Be firm and you will overcome the problems. Weakness and passivity will increase them.

You will realise a long-felt social ambition.

You are soon to put on your best clothes and set out on a joyous journey.

A very good omen.

Money and exotic gifts are on the way.

A dreadful omen. You may be involved in a scene of physical violence which will bring death to at least one person.

Vanity and extravagance are going to lead to ruin.

Someone will die within a year, and the manner of their death will be very strange and mysterious. Remember this!

A **B**

Tropical lands, the Equator, and blazing passions soon enter your destiny.

A cable or telegram will bring you important news on which you must make a hasty decision. Do not fear!

All that is hostile to you will be destroyed.

You are going to be visited by a number of people – one of them an attractive stranger.

Journeys are profitable, but they must be made swiftly.

Someone who is supposed to be an ally will prove to be working for your enemies.

A wonderful omen. You are going to be a happy mortal!

A bad omen. Expect the worst. Lie low.

Tears and frustrations; you are going to be let down.

Ideogram No. XXIV

The stars are about to assume very favourable aspects.

A lucky omen. Your prospects are magnificent.

Something hidden will be brought to light.

Some delusive mirage is beckoning you.

If it's luck you need, 'tis luck you'll get.

A major need is going to be supplied.

Fevers of mind and body. Rest as comfortably as possible, and wait for recovery.

A bad omen. New measures of any sort should be delayed.

You may be accused of something you have not done, or implicated in a scandal.

News of ill health.

A   B

You are being too open and confiding: keep your thoughts to yourself.

There is trouble for you with documents and papers. Don't sign anything without great care.

A good omen for business matters. Your career is going to move ahead.

A herald of good news is coming to your door.

Unhappy events must be expected.

A dark and sinister omen. You will hear of some very bad news affecting others.

If you feel your life is at a standstill, just wait: destiny is preparing great things for you.

Happiness is going to fill your heart, and each day will bring new delight.

Either marriage or children or both are certain for you within a year.

A heavy sorrow is coming.

Strained relations with another person may lead to an outburst. Stay clear of such a person, or you will be sorry.

You are lacking foresight. Be more thoughtful about your decisions and actions.

Your vitality is low. You need change of scene and rest.

A   B

You should take medical advice.

A very happy time in company with other people: don't refuse an invitation or hold back.

Good news about money and a love affair.

A bad omen.

Cast on the 1st, 5th, 11th or 17th of the month, a lucky omen. On other days, take warning of misfortune.

Prepare for a difficult time ahead.

Sensual gratifications are on the way. You will have much pleasure.

Beware of a false promise. Don't build on it.

A dispute is going to arise over documents and the written word.

Ideogram No. XXV

A **B**

You are going to be tied up in knots by a good-looking person, most likely a redhead.

Those who are rejoicing in their wealth and feel secure in their pride – beware! Those who are poor and sad – take comfort!

You are in danger of committing a serious indiscretion.

You will have to postpone a number of plans for the time being.

For the poor, very good news is at hand. For the rich – the shadow of ruin draws near.

If you are unattached, you are soon going to be deep in a love affair. The volcano of passion is about to erupt. . . .!

Expect to lose valuables or loose sums of money.

Danger of being menaced, or tied up and robbed.

An omen which will ensure you much happiness in the coming year.

You will hear of something very odd, which will give you quite a surprise.

A	**B**	
		Physical danger threatens. When it looms, remember and either run or take cover – don't try to be a hero.
		Your stars are not friendly, so take care.
		You may expect to have sad news.
		Advancement, recognition of services rendered.
		A favourable settlement in or out of court.
		Danger of riots, vandalism and looting.
		Be cautious. Any kind of recklessness will end in a serious accident.
		A bad omen. Money drains away like water through a sieve. Danger of giving in to blackmail.
		A wedding and a funeral will follow close on one another.
		Your desire for pleasure is going to get you into trouble.
		A journey and a great effort – alas – all to no purpose.
		Enemies, who seem strong and likely to get the upper hand, will be routed and destroyed.
		A gift will be given you, but it presages a farewell.

A   B

Valuable objects and jewels are to be yours.

You are to own a great deal of property, and your house will be crammed with costly and luxurious things.

Do not count on your good fortune – just when it seems to be at its best, it will evaporate.

Illness and anxieties are to be expected.

You do not at present merit good fortune. Change your ways!

Your goods may be seized and your property mortgaged. Quick thinking may prevent it.

A bad omen.

You are going to be the centre of an unpleasant incident.

Ideogram No. XXVI

A   **B**

Not a good omen, but you will get by somehow.

The sea and seaside are not lucky to you.

You are the unwitting victim of a plot to rob you or ruin your reputation, and make you flee into exile.

You will soon have news that will make you happy.

Gifts from admirers, declarations of physical attraction.

A health condition is going to improve beyond expectation.

A good time for making a profit. In any case, a stroke of luck is on the way.

All troubles are about to vanish miraculously.

A very good omen, foretelling happiness in love, luck with money and solid tokens of friendship.

You will be rewarded for a good deed of which you are unaware.

133

A   B

If times are hard, help is on the way. For the rich and successful – people are out to destroy you.

A bad omen. Decisions and actions at this time must be carefully thought out.

Cast on the 13th of the month – sudden news of death. Other days, serious illness.

For matters connected with entertaining or dealing with the public, a wonderful omen. Applause and praise!

A long-hidden skeleton will fall out of its closet.

Someone you dislike is going to be hit by scandal.

Riches, public recognition, and a high place in the world are to be yours.

You should take trouble to make the best of yourself, and will win a high opinion where it counts.

Someone who has hurt you will receive a sudden blow from Fate.

News of great joy, invitations and brilliant society.

You are too trusting. You believe someone likes you who in fact hates you.

A relative or close friend is going to die suddenly.

You are going to be led among very bad people. Have nothing to do with them.

A   B

You are going to have the opportunity of acquiring a great deal of money. Think well before you take it.

What you most wish for at this very moment you will obtain within a short time.

You are going to have sad news and a serious problem.

Great difficulties are impending. Not much can be done.

Cast on a Sunday: a romantic encounter. On Monday: inconstant lovers. On Wednesday: bribes. On Friday: an admirer will pursue you. The rest of the week: your lover will cost you money.

You are likely to have trouble over something you have written.

If you are trying to join a society or club, you will have trouble. Avoid social issues, as these are under adverse stars.

Beware of an attractive man. He wants your body and your money too.

A serious problem which hangs over you is going to be happily solved.

135

Ideogram No. XXVII

A   B

Nothing stands still. Expect much activity and with it good fortune.

You and others will have cause for rejoicing in the near future.

If things are not going well, look forward to a sudden and happy change in your stars.

You must not rely on others. They will disappoint you. Be proud and independent.

You are going to get help from a person in a position of influence. Money problems will be solved.

Expect delay and inaction. It is an unprofitable season.

Money is coming to you, according to your needs.

Whatever you are about to do will succeed.

Something disturbing and worrying is about to happen which may affect you indirectly.

Misunderstandings. Silence is golden.

A B

An unlucky omen except on the third of the month or any date that is a multiple of three, when it is good.

Cast on a Monday: a new friend will be made. On a Tuesday: beware of someone you are going to meet.

Happy times ahead, with reunions and pleasant surprises.

If everything seems carefree and all is gaiety, beware – there may be a phantom at the feast!

A surprise wedding or union between two people, one known to you.

A sad farewell will soon be said, and a good influence will leave your life forever.

Invitations and much social activity.

A very lucky omen.

A change of address is coming for you very soon.

Unexpected and surprising news is on the way.

Your affairs are about to take an upward turn, and you will be very pleased indeed.

You are about to meet someone who will become quite important in your life.

A very lucky omen. A good time to make positive decisions.

A   B

Expect ill health – especially of a mental or nervous origin.

A bad omen. There is a dark cloud on the horizon.

Watch for your reputation, especially if your pleasures are likely to endanger it.

Stagnation and delays. Nothing moves forward.

News of especial interest is on the way.

You have the opportunity to rise in life – but it will cause envy and you will not be liked for it.

News of a funeral.

At the end of a journey – yours or someone else's – a meeting is to take place which will be to your mutual satisfaction.

You are not giving of your best or behaving as you ought.

138

Ideogram No. XXVIII

A B

Promotion is in the air. You will hear of honours being bestowed – if not on you, then on one you care about.

However unlikely, be sure that money is on the way to solve pressing financial needs.

An omen which says 'Your undertakings will be fruitless this time. Try again.'

Your stars are hostile, so expect difficulties.

News of birth, deliverance, release, relief.

You are about to cross 'the bridge of flowers' – a new and happier chapter is to begin.

All money dealings will have good results, the bolder the business the better.

Beware! This is a dreadful omen.

You have a secret enemy. You have done them no harm but they work against you.

You may find yourself in trouble, but take courage, you will get yourself out of it.

A   **B**

Expect a reverse or upset of plans.

The air buzzes with rumour and gossip, nothing is certain, and you had best take measures for your safety.

A wonderful omen. Riches, rejoicing, success, honours, valuable gifts, all are at your feet.

Not a happy time for lovers; quarrels are certain.

Within two months, expect the death of someone who is important to you.

Take action against those who oppose you. You must now either rise or fall through your determination, or lack of it.

All your material needs are about to be met.

Quarrels over property and money.

You are about to be singled out for the bestowal of some special privilege or honour.

Very bad news – but you will be saved from harm.

This omen presages the sad ending of a friendship or association.

You will have to defer plans and postpone meetings.

A strange, miraculous event is about to take place, in which the intervention of Invisible Powers will be seen.

A   B

You are subject to depression and your thoughts are confused.

A bad omen.

Someone is determined to destroy you. This is a ruthless and crafty enemy.

Cast on a Sunday: gifts. On Thursday: money loss. On Saturday: sexuality and sexual experiences.

Be humble! You are going to eat the bread of humiliation.

A good omen, especially for money matters, examinations and hopes of admission to colleges, clubs, etc.

You are about to spend money, time and energy – in vain.

You will soon encounter much kindness and goodness of heart, from someone who is a friend worth having.

Amorous encounters, romantic escapades, secret meetings in a discreet rendezvous.

Ideogram No. XXIX

A   **B**

A death will cause some important changes round you.

A disappointment in love or business may be expected. Ambition will be frustrated, at least for the time.

Nothing will go right until your next birthday.

A bad omen.

A very lucky conjunction of stars may be expected soon. You will enjoy the friendship and patronage of great people.

Spend money, and you will get money.

Someone very untrustworthy is about – give them no keys or confidences.

A woman is going to be troublesome.

A strange discovery will be made.

You are going to be unexpectedly busy, so don't expect a rest.

A	B	
		Someone who says 'yes' means 'no'.
		You are likely to be cheated over money.
		A very lucky omen.
		You are going to enjoy yourself.
		Troubles for a friend are on the way.
		You should cultivate someone's acquaintance.
		Great diplomacy is necessary with someone you are associated with.
		You are soon going to change your address.
		Vital forces are likely to be low, so take things quietly.
		Be cautious in your decisions and actions.
		Something disagreeable is about to take place.
		You are being too open; candour is an excellent quality, but discretion is sometimes necessary.
		In the next week, expect some good news, some money, but also some misunderstandings.

A B

Good harvests, great profit, worthwhile enterprises are in your path.

Someone is going to do you a very good turn.

Marriage is in the air, approved of by all.

A very happy omen.

Happy social occasions, enjoyment without anxiety.

The next month brings a host of annoyances, but then all will go very well indeed.

Take care of accidents of the road.

You are being impatient. Persevere at a slow pace.

An unlucky omen.

Ideogram No. XXX

A   **B**

Something of value is coming your way. A good time for planning a journey, which will work out well.

Your situation is going to improve, in spite of your fears.

A bad omen. Count on nothing and nobody.

Expect a disappointment.

Good luck is on the way. Your ambitions of the present time will be realised.

Very good fortune is ahead.

For a man, this omen presages a wealthy patron; for a woman, a rich admirer.

You are entering a maze, but will emerge with ease.

Keep clear of difficult situations.

Don't get involved with legal matters. Be subtle with officials.

A	B	
		Health seems not too good at present; just take things quietly.
		Expect unhappiness and complications in your personal life.
		A bad omen.
		All your enterprises are going to succeed.
		Illness and misfortune are going to be overcome – either for yourself or persons near to you.
		Not a good time for business or journeys.
		The one you desire will be yours.
		You will find a door opens for you, and you will receive a welcome invitation.
		An omen of troubles and affliction.
		Your path lies uphill all the way, and nobody is going to help – but go on bravely.
		New means of making money are going to be revealed. New friends will give you self-confidence.
		A very good omen. Go forward boldly.
		You may expect to be lucky. If you are stepping out into the blue, you will land on your feet.

A   B

You are going to be able to do as you please, and leave your cares aside for quite some time.

Your projects are shadowed by misfortune; your relationships are going to become difficult.

Be especially careful about plans or preparations. This is a time for caution.

A good time for a big investment.

Expect to be reunited with someone you know, and miss.

Relatives, friends and associates are going to have troubles with which you will be indirectly burdened.

A marriage is in the air – more a marriage of convenience than of love.

You are going to lose a friend; expect marked coldness and then hostility.

You are going to hear some bad news. Be prepared!

Ideogram No. XXXI

A   **B**

A time of disappointment and depression. There is nothing you can do about it, so wait for things to improve.

There are evil forces at work: they will soon be out in the open.

You want one thing but will get another – you start on one path and find yourself somewhere you didn't expect to be.

If you have troubles, a good angel is going to banish them.

Someone quite important is going to be very useful to you.

Expect stings, bites, scratches – be careful of food in a restaurant.

You are not very strong at present and there is danger of virus infections.

An omen which foretells general good fortune, and brings you the support of friends and strangers.

Have nothing to do with a shady project or venture. Bad company will bring you harm.

A troublesome omen. Your stars are at sixes and sevens.

A **B**

This omen foretells feminine health troubles, visits to clinic and matters concerning pregnancies. For a pregnant woman, a difficult time.

You are going to be involved in something which will tarnish your reputation if you don't take care.

A bad omen.

Alcohol, drugs, diet and medicines should all be treated warily at this time, as there is danger from any of them.

Excellent omen for new undertakings and family matters.

Misunderstandings among friends. Try to make a new friend and it just will not work out.

You want a new home or to make big changes in your present home – all your hopes will soon be realised.

Gain in business matters, repayment of debts, increase in value of property.

You are in for rather a lean time – it will do you no great harm.

Very good news is on the way, and you will get some material benefit.

You are building castles in the air.

Do not commit yourself in an important matter related to your career.

Before a year is out you will visit a strange land in strange circumstances.

A B

You are going to have a unique opportunity to make money – grasp it, for it will soon pass.

A very lucky omen. Nothing bad, and some good, will happen for maybe a year.

You will encourage a very good match between two people well suited to each other. If you are trying to win the favour of someone, you will succeed.

A good time for lovers.

For a woman, a man who says he loves you will get what he wants and then leave you. For a man, don't be deceived by a pretty face.

You are going to be attracted to someone who will be really bad for you.

An attractive young man or woman is going to fall in love with someone much older.

Take care! This is a bad time for money matters.

You must deal with others very carefully or you will make a serious mistake.

150

Ideogram No. XXXII

A B

Someone is going to tell you untrue gossip and try to change your opinion – pay no heed.

Be calm. You are liable to lose your temper – and you will be sorry for it.

A good time for business or getting promotion or honours.

All is change, change, change – nothing stands still and do not expect to see the end result of it all.

You are going to have a lucky escape from misfortune and however close to disaster you come, you will be successful.

Something you do or say may be misunderstood with very bad results for you and others.

Any connection you may have with trade will suddenly become very successful.

Try to be more active in your community life – you are needed there!

Someone who pretends great friendship for you is out to make use of you in some way: you will find out soon.

If you think that everything is now going to be easy – think again. You will have to strive!

A B

Someone is being very slow in making up their mind about you. Be patient.

A very important person will become your close friend.

A great passion will soon fade and die. A bad time for love and enthusiasm.

You will soon cultivate a new interest which will give you much pleasure and even profit.

You will leave a substantial fortune when you die – which won't be for a long time.

Opposition in what you want to achieve will be overcome – even if what you want is only peace of mind.

Many of your values need rethinking before you can know true happiness.

Life is a test of endurance. Endure and keep smiling.

Value what is near at hand; fulfil yourself with things within your horizons.

News of sudden death or an unmarried girl who becomes a mother.

Expect ingratitude.

Nothing comes easily at this time, and everything is ups and downs.

You would like to be someone's friend – don't delude yourself.

152

A   **B**

Consulted on a Tuesday, this omen is good, but on other days it presages a defeat.

Don't complicate your life just now. Keep things simple and all will be well.

You are going to be in some kind of danger, but you will get over it.

A very lucky omen.

An ardent lover is about to appear on the scene.

Deceit in matters of the heart.

Your beloved thinks only of you. If you have no love life at present, expect a surprise.

Family and personal matters are troublesome, and will become more so.

Friendship and love are in the air, and so is expenditure – you may enjoy the former, but avoid the latter.

Four: Sand Divining

Egypt has the oldest tourist industry in the world. The ancient Greeks visited its marvels and pondered on its mysteries; the Emperor Hadrian sailed up the Nile as far as the cataracts in a fleet of golden-prowed yachts.

Egypt is an inexhaustible well of wonders. Even in what are to us ancient times, the Egyptians were ever trying to unravel the more ancient secrets of the temples, and also to possess themselves of their treasures. In about 100 B.C., during the Ptolemaic era, a demotic papyrus put into English verse by Gilbert Murray tells how Setne, a High Priest of Ptah, explored the hypogea with which Egypt is honeycombed for the Book of Thoth, known as the Emerald Table, after the green marble or malachite temple in the groves of Memphis where it had been enshrined.

> That night they found the tomb, and AN-HERU
> Stayed at the door, but SETNE passing through
> On seven great doors and seven windings spake
> His spells and found the room; and all was true.

The Copts, the Egyptians monophysite Christians whose church is the first of Christendom, preserve many of the ancient customs in their traditions, and the ancient language in their liturgy. The largest percentage of the rest of the Egyptian people are in fact Islamised Copts, although their Christian compatriots have been less subject to the influences of population movement. Century after century, certain classes of Egyptian, often unlettered, but learning their arts orally from their fathers, have amused the tourists as guides, snake charmers, baboon trainers and fortune tellers.

The principal means they employ is sand divination, and, if the manner in which it is practised varies from one locality to another, the essentials are the same. Whether the solemn practitioner in robe and cloak is found in Alexandria, Cairo, Assiut or Luxor, his predictions are based on that geomantic formation of patterns, meaningful to the diviner, which is the foundation of all forms of seership except those making use of pure clairvoyance, trance or magic.

Today the Nile temples are silent, although awe-inspiring and numinous as ever. Only at Abydos do the prayers to Osiris still faintly echo through the vast colonnades at sunset and dawn, recited by an elderly Englishwoman who has appointed herself guardian of the fane, has lived close by for many years, and passes her days and often nights there.

The mysteries of the temples may to some extent be deciphered by anyone with a knowledge of the hieroglyphic alphabet, but there is more still to be learned in the daily life of the Egyptians, to be sifted out by the seeker who takes the trouble to learn Arabic. Knowledge of the occult sciences must be sadly incomplete for the student not acquainted with the Arabic language which has, more than any other, cherished the profound lore of the past.

What follows is an outline of sand divination as it is known in Egypt, and as it has been practised there for many centuries. The diviners usually know only as much of several foreign languages as will enable them to say what the oracle imparts. It may be possible to elaborate; here it is given in its bare essentials. Possible, too, that the oracle could be adapted to lines drawn upon a sheet of paper. This is for the amateur to decide, although the way the lines are drawn in the sand, their depth and general appearance, seems meaningful to the diviner. In Europe, sand divination may perhaps be best left for a visit to the beach. Smooth earth or gravel might suit but somehow seems lacking in the savour and associate quality of the original. If not already provided with a riding whip or parasol the querent is handed a cane and asked to make any number of random lines in the sand within arm's reach of the spot where he is standing or sitting.

Example:
A

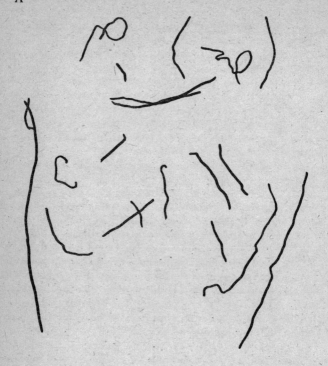

The practitioner keeps in his head a simple diagram which has been ingrained there from childhood. A good memory and a vivid pictorial imagination seem often to compensate for a lack of schooling. The diagram learned by the sand diviner is this:

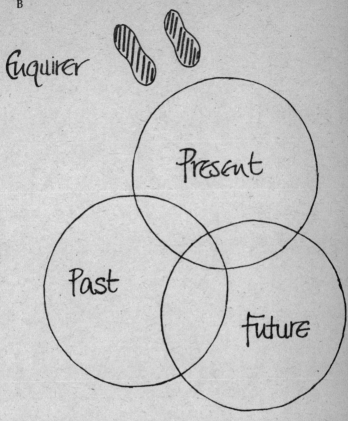

The circle nearest to the enquirer the present; that to his right is the past: that furthest from him the future. The three circles are interlinked.

Diagram C shows the imposition of the lines in A upon the three circles in B.

Example:
    C

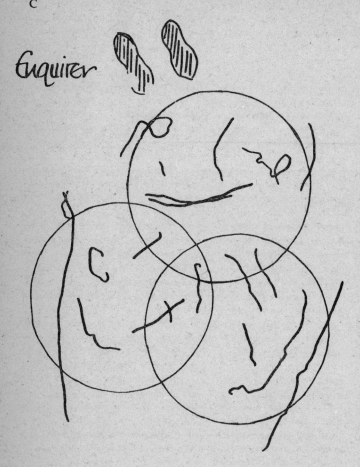

Unless the diviner is possessed of a vivid pictorial imagination, it is better to draw the three circles on the ground before making a start. By using the Key, the following interpretation of the above example would be given.

In the circle of the Past, the line on the far left crosses the circle in two places and means that the enquirer has had a chance of great good fortune but has lost it. The circle of the Present shows a curved line crossing the perimeter; this is a line of accident, to be expected in the near future, but which will not prove serious. Had it crossed into the circle of the Future, the after-effects would be prolonged and perhaps severe: had it entered the circle and shot out again at a tangent, the accident would be a very serious one. However, if the circle of the Future contains plenty of lines, the normal prolongation of this present life is to be hoped for.

A line moving away from the enquirer in circle 1, and having a pothook at its end turning to the right, means that good fortune may be expected at about the present time. Another right-turning line in the Past shows that the enquirer has indeed had great opportunities which have been wasted.

The four lines crossing circle 1 and lying also in circles 2 and 3 show that there is a genuine effort now being made to improve things, and that this effort will be rewarded. The long line in circle 3, which twice changes course and ends with a little pothook, indicates that in later life there will be a great love affair. The two small lines in circles 1 and 3 indicate that the enquirer is likely to have two children, one born in a year or so of the divination, another some years ahead.

The hooked line cutting circles 1 and 3 indicates some wise financial thinking which will ensure the security of old age. The odd, wavy line in circle 1 means much travel. The cross, with its longest line crossing the perimeter of circle 3, shows that the enquirer cannot be truly happy in the married state and is seeking freedom: one marriage will end in divorce.

The long line in circle 3, which cuts it in two places, indicates that a good old age will be reached and that death will come suddenly. In the past, someone whose name begins with a C has meant much to the enquirer: this person will be met with again. The circle and line moving away from circle 1, near the enquirer, shows that there will soon be a desired change of residence which will enhance the general life-style.

Accidents. Curved lines, crossing the perimeter of any of the circles, having their greatest length outside the circle. Dangerous accidents are shown by such a line crossing two of the circles.

Children. Small, straight lines within the circles.

Good Fortune. Lines within the circles, ending in pothooks away from the enquirer and to his right. Any line cutting a circle is a line of good fortune missed. Where such a line pertaining to the present is crossed by lines entering any of the other circles, reasonable stability may be expected in the material sense. Exceptional good fortune is denoted by a line cutting the perimeters of all three circles. Where more than one such line exists, the enquirer will rise to the greatest heights, and if such lines extend well beyond the circles, then the kind of fame which brings immortality may be expected.

Health. Small stones or grit in the areas where the circles do not interlink show health problems.

Legal matters. Barbed lines or lines criss-crossed with smaller ones.

Love. Long, wavy lines within a circle, the stronger and more definite their appearance, the stronger the attachment.

Marriage (or important liaisons). Shown by crosses. If a cross is clear of the interlinked parts of the circles, then a marriage will endure; if one of its lines crosses any circle, it will end. In the given example, it would seem that that marriage cross starts in the past, crosses the line of the future, and is therefore impermanent. Marriage crosses in the intersection of the circles are not lasting.

Money. Hooked lines with the pothook closest to the enquirer and with the line ending away from him, and crossing any of the overlapping perimeters, indicate wise financial or business thinking, and that enterprises will succeed. Dark pebbles or grit in the areas where the circles interlink denote the acquisition of property or land. Where such lines are absent, fears for the enquirer's material future may be entertained.

Names and initials. when a mark is made resembling an initial or name, this is taken into account and the name or initial given to the enquirer.

Travel. Confused, squirming lines.

Tridents. A trident shape, anywhere within the circle 1, 2 or 3, pointing towards the enquirer, means that he is his own worst enemy, and needs to change the way of thought and life. A trident whose points are away from the enquirer foretells applause and public adulation. A long line crossing the circles of the present or future, or both, beginning well outside the circles, and ending more or less in the centre of one of them, gives rise to fear of danger, either from physical attack or self-inflicted.

The line furthest from the enquirer, in the circle of the future, if traversing the perimeter at two points, indicates sudden death. No such line indicates a normal life span. A line going straight away from close to the enquirer's feet, and crossing the outer edge of circles 2 or 3 at the point furthest from the enquirer means news of sudden death or an unexpected shock.

Lines may be linked to one another, and with experience their inter-relationship may be read. For example, a marriage and a success line joined together would mean a marriage bringing wealth or good connections.

The main thing is that all means of divination should be stimulating and interesting enough for the diviner to 'get something' from them. Some natural psychics are 'turned on' by one kind of stimulus but not another – for example, may be good with Tarot cards, but not with the lines of the hand. Traditional, received meanings are interesting and important, or course, but the developing psychic should always be asking 'What does this or this mean to ME? Someone who has been looking for years for the right instrument might suddenly find an affinity with sand and develop the technique in an inimitable way.

Five: Becoming your own Sibyl

Nineteenth and Twentieth Century western men have not on the whole been inclined to release their psychic energies. The number of children who say 'Daddy I want to be a fortune teller when I grow up' cannot be large. University courses in the subject are hard to find, and reliable teachers, among the small advertisements in psychic journals, even more so. As a lad I was tempted to send a stamped, addressed envelope to a veiled figure holding out a crystal ball, shown in an advertisement hailing from California, and who promised total mastery of the secrets of the Universe. I did not do so: possessor of a vein of scepticism which has not made for comfort but has stood me in good stead.

However, it is an occult maxim that the seeker will inevitably find – though not always what he thinks he is looking for – and an insatiable curiosity is the first requisite of the incipient psychic who vaguely realises that he or she wants to get into training. For present help, there has been, over recent years, a flood of popular literature on these matters; sensationalised by publishers whose naivety is equalled only by the capacity for plagiarism of their authors who are in general the type of person who is ready to jump aboard any band wagon that happens by. Still, for those who want them, the desired aids for psychic unfolding will sift through the subtle byways of the mind, will stick there, and stay, tiny lucent particles slowly forming into pearls of great price. It is inclined to be a slow process, although it can be assisted by sundry techniques old and new, tried and fairly true.

There is always someone, eventually, to point the way. Gurus are generally associated with metaphysical areas not necessarily linked with the psychic – it is probable that many individuals who spend entire days and nights standing on their heads, or contemplating the Seventeen Hinayanas or whatever, are hopeless at ESP or lively conversations with their potted sweetheart vine.

In our day, the guru's functions, not to speak of the priest's and inquisitor's, have been to some extent taken over by the biologist, the physicist, the bio-chemist, not to speak of the anthropologist and executives in parasite industries like sociology, who in spite of their tendency to rigidity are in however small a degree compelled by powers invisible to serve the cause of a higher Intelligence whose patient insistence will not be denied.

Many seekers spend their lives looking vainly for a real, authentic, fully tested and operative guru, which to them means a person of ascetic and venerable aspect, the kind of person you see in health stores, and if possible the possessor of an ample white beard and some kind of flowing robe. It must be said here and now that these are in short supply, and although I have in the past done my share of looking for what I imagined to be the genuine article, it gradually dawned on me that gurus usually come in unlikely guises and may be discovered in improbable places. A jolly, extrovert Franciscan monk, from Brittany and therefore having a touch of the druidic: a shabby, unpunctual little official at the Iranian Ministry of Information – oh yes, he was a real, genuine, authentic Sufi Master – : a wiry, sunburnt English engineer who had spent all his life in the service of British India: all these were gurus in the true sense of the word and are remembered and venerated as such by those who know them. Their names? Masters do not understand about public recognition.

Scientists of various shapes and sizes have studied forms of divination and other psychic activity with some attention in recent years. Where a diviner or seer 'does it himself', for example makes a pencil jump or scrutinises whatever is the chosen instrument of scrutiny, whether a sheep's liver or a plastikrystal ball, and then authoritatively gives his findings, attempts at analysis are at their most faltering. Obviously the famous X type of energy is called for, and that certain states of mind come into operation, different from the states of mind you have to be in to run the affairs of your daily life, and which are 'switched on' in different ways.*

* The editor of the *News of the World* women's pages, Unity Hall, told me she has noticed that psychics are inclined to use similes and metaphors of an electrical nature.

Some authors have warned against seership by individuals to satisfy their own curiosity, but what mental activity of any sort can take place without difficulties and dangers? Where superstition and derangement are active, psychism is not necessarily active along with them, although mental hospitals witness very odd feats which the professionals in charge prefer to ignore.

The gap between psychic activity, superstition and derangement may be extremely narrow; yet neither can psychism blossom in a bland, bran-and-water, prescriptive or materialist mental climate – although it is amazing what it can and will do in the unfriendliest of environments.

The French occultist, Papus, described ably the problems faced by personalities feeling the urge to develop psychically but in whom some categories of detrimental characteristics predominate. Other thinkers like Steiner have described these categories in slightly different terms; all of them are present simultaneously to some degree in nearly everyone: in numerous individuals where one of the four 'centres' is over-reacting there is a proportionate increase in psychic 'blocks'.

The 'instinctive' centre when overstated produces idleness, excessive appetites, and inertia. The exaggeration of the 'centre' of sensibility tends to produce sensuality and falsehood, hostility and aggression. The exaggeration of the intellectual 'centre' produces gnawing resentments and envy. The over-activation of the will produces despotism, ambition and pride. Exaggeration of masculinity or femininity in turn produce exaggerations counter-active to psychic development.

In particular, the intellectual has more to overcome because possessed of a greater reasoning power and cultural development which incline to turn the intellectual away from the street, the salon, the café, and anywhere seething humanity is found in all its glory and pathos, and to create a refuge in some ivory tower moated with dogmatism.

Tripping, Smoking etc.

There is a good deal of discussion about the use of narcotics and hallucinogens in sharpening psychism. At the present time, drugs capable of widening and altering consciousness are too closely associated with gratuitous experience and escapism to have a general value in assisting psychic growth. On balance, the negative effects outweigh the positive, and until the use of drugs is considered to be sacramental no responsible person would wish to recommend them in this context. It is hard enough for most of us to discover and live in our personal reality by means of the data of daily life: yet it is this which is the prime requirement for the wakening psyche.

All voyages of exploration, it may be argued, are worth the while. In the continent of the psychedelic and the altered state of consciousness there have been both notable discoveries and gallant sacrifices made by brave and reckless beings: yet the charts are too obscure, and the means of arrival and return so far too debatable. But astronauts of consciousness will nevertheless continue to prepare, and gradually more highly skilled techniques will become available to assist them.

Talismans

If you have been given a love locket or a friendship bracelet you have received a talisman. You possess a talisman if you wear a cross, a Star of David, a hammer and sickle, or a badge bearing some legend such as Peaches Here's Your Can. Talismans can be powerful or loving, dedicatory to a higher purpose or to vanity and folly. They do not have to be worn upon the person. My own is a photograph twelve inches high, glazed and with a heavy gilt and wood frame, which would require an individual a good deal taller and stronger than myself to make a pendant out of it.

Talismans which have been magnetised magically are something special. An aware person cannot mistake such an object when placed in the hand. An ancient Egyptian example in the possession of an Upper Egyptian family, who are glad to demonstrate its properties, has a mosquito beautifully engraved on the quartz medallion: no insect will settle on or sting the wearer. These things must puzzle the logically minded: we are approaching an era when they will become explicable.

The talisman may be a gift, be acquired in strange circumstances, or have a special association or use. In the latter category one may almost place the pendulums and rods of the dowser, who like many craftsmen forms a special relationship with his tools. A sure way of acquiring a talisman is by having something come to hand at a moment of special stress or significance. The properties of a talisman are special to it and to the possessor; at least a disposition to believe in those properties seems necessary for it to work.

An excellent way of getting a talisman, recommended by the magical profession, is to set out for a walk in a random direction, to walk until so weary that you say to yourself 'I MUST stop for a rest', and, stopping at this moment, you pick up the first small object you see. In magical practice, these operations are governed by the planets, but in this one there is no need to puzzle over the *ephemeris*, although it would be a good thing if you were to do it during the month of your birth sign. There are seasons when we are more efficient, brighter, stronger; the star-lore of the ancients was a factual science.

If you are going to have a pendant made of your pebble, shell, or beer bottle top, then you must pay for it with your own money. Magical gifts must be unsolicited, but if you are doing something like this you must pay for it yourself. If you want to keep your talisman in a little bag, then you must stitch it with your own hands, preferably from a piece of fabric you already possess, and made of silk, wool or linen.

Divination with the Talismans

A number of the walks as described above will get you a nice collection of odds and ends and will also do you good. Or, if your first walk is on a beach or stony place, you may be able to sit yourself down and make a collection then and there, perhaps a dozen, maybe more. However, if you are going to use your talismans for the kind of divination described below, you will want little objects which will roll and scatter fairly well, although they need not be of like size or colour: better indeed if they provide some contrasts.

Clean your pebbles (or whatever) carefully, and put them in their bag. When you have some free time, and are alone, and quiet, sit on the floor and spill your pebbles out of the bag. Incidentally, by quiet I mean quiet; large numbers of people today are so accustomed to the radio, the television and other instruments continually blaring that they have forgotten what silence is, or are frightened of it. Some magical or mystical operations require forms of rhythmic accompaniment. Generally, silence is best. The singing of birds and the miaowing of cats (perhaps not both together) are always permissible, while a feline presence is psychically stimulating. Dogs, I am afraid, on the other hand . . . but I do not wish to offend those who love these creatures as much as life itself.

The pebbles will scatter hither and thither. Look at them and their relationship with one another. Remember the lines of the good old man in the forest in *As You Like it*: 'Books in the running brooks, sermons in stones. . .' Maybe some of the stones have got together in a little group and look like a group of people. Or do they more closely resemble a sum of money? These stones seem to have formed a barricade or obstacle, and that one there, is it facing the obstacle, looking as though it were going to pass through, or is it rushing away from it? Here are two pebbles, much alike, and close together: lovers, maybe? Or a figure of eight, the alchemical symbol for rest in the midst of movement and change? Have the stones fallen in rather a confused hotpotch, with just three or four in a line moving away, or perhaps towards the mass? Perhaps the end pebble in the line is wanting to go off on a journey, leaving all that confusion behind? Or is it approaching the mass of pebbles, determined to become involved with them?

Maybe you have some very dark-coloured pebbles and you will, after playing with them a few times, decide that these represent people in general. Perhaps you will have a black and a white, which will come to mean a man and a woman. This reddish one, now, the colour of Mars, will you make it symbolise conflicts? This one, with golden streaks, might come to stand for money. Here is one for love, and another for health . . . or quite possibly you won't have this approach at all, and any of the pebbles will have meaning only in relationship with the others.

Like the Egyptian sand divination we described previously, you may feel you need some sort of blueprint or diagram on which you or whoever consults you can shake and roll the pebbles. It would be really nice if you could be bold enough not to use it, and to rely confidently upon your developing intuition and imagination, but if you feel you must, then here is something for you to work with.

Material gain but no delight	News of Death	News of Birth	Abundance	Union	Travel to the East	
Gold and treasure	obey the law or you will be in trouble	Cheer up! All will be well	JOY IN ALL YOUR	insignificant	An evil woman	of craft, guile and passions
An evil man	If you can behold All will be well	You are going to start a new life	SUCCESS AND	ENTERPRISES.	insignificant	Beware your own worst enemy
Travel to the North	Hospitals and doctors	Travel to the West	Harmony	Peace	insignificant	You are your own worst enemy
Health is in danger	Lawsuits and lawyers	Surprising news of money	You are truely loved	You will win the one you love	insignificant	
A good woman	The cup of pleasure is being filled	Your mind is confused - be more thoughtful	News of birth	News of Death	Love will bring obligations	
You are moving in the wrong direction	A strange woman is meeting you - be strange + true	Evil things surround you - be thoughtful	Take heed - folly and extravagance	A old person will do you a good turn	Travel to the South	You have your desire but it will do you no good

The above chart may be simplified or rendered more complex. It should be about 2 metres square, to allow for a free scattering of the pebbles. The oracle obtained will be in response to a situation typical of the moment or very near at hand. The principal object of the oracle is not in fact to tell somebody something, but to make you more percipient, so do not be dismayed if your results are at first not very hopeful. Many will be astonished at their oracular abilities. Practice is the best way to improvement.

Dowsing and Healing

Both dowsing and healing are manifestations of psychic energy, and many more people possess the potential to practise them than might be supposed.

168

The pendulums and divining rods may be made to suit individual taste. Rods of hazel, whalebone or any flexible material will do. Some people swear by rods made from wire coathangers. A pendulum consists of any light weight suspended from a strong thread and held between the thumb and forefinger or any other way that seems right for the individual operator. Divining can be used for discovering underground water, metals or anything else the diviner may be consciously looking for. The pendulum can be used over maps to discover the whereabouts of missing persons: it may be guessed that to have a dowser in the family could be an embarrassment for anyone inclined to prevaricate about their movements.

In dowsing, the subjective imagination is a constant bugbear. If you are looking for something and start 'wishing' a degree too strongly that what you are looking for might be near at hand, then the wish will not only be father to the thought but the pendulum will start to swing or the rod to twitch in an illusory pantomime of discovery!

To agree on a glossary of pendulum movements for dowsers would be impossible, for rods and pendulums seem to have their own way of setting about the work with each individual. However, so many practical results are recorded each day with these instruments it is impossible to under-estimate their value as well as their potential. In dowsing we certainly see a natural energy and capacity closely intertwined with personal mental processes, a phenomenon still waiting for further explanation. Meanwhile, the British Society of Dowsers continues its pioneering endeavours, and acts as a commonsensical, good-humoured spearhead in the cause of psychic awareness. For the developing psychic, a course in dowsing is recommended, for if you are capable of psychic work at all, you should be able to dowse after a little practice.

Apart from water divining, the most familiar kind of dowsing is determination of the sex of eggs and unborn animals and humans. Not all of us have access to fertile eggs, and although pregnant ladies are usually interested to have this experiment performed upon them, the time factor as well as the number of subjects conveniently available at once would make other tests more desirable for the novice.

A good one, recommended by members of the British Society of

Dowsers, is to sit with the pendulum poised over an electric light flex, with the lamp either covered or led into another room so that the switching on and off of the bulb does not affect the subjective imagination. A second party controls the switch, neither seen nor heard by the dowser, who should get a positive swing when the current is on, and negative when it is off. The way the pendulum swings in both instances will teach the individual his own positive and negative pendulum movement.

The late Lt. Col. F.A. Archdale, a notable worker in the field of radiesthesia, recommended the following test for an individual's sensitivity.

'Stand erect, facing due West. Relax as much as possible, place the left hand over the solar plexus, palm inward with the fingers closed. Suspend the pendulum from the right hand, using the full length of the twine, so that the pendulum is opposite the centre of the left hand and about eight inches from it. The pendulum will commence to gyrate in a clockwise direction. Count the number of gyrations carefully, and if the gyrations are weak and less than fifteen your chances of getting any reliable results from radiesthesia are remote and I suggest you go no further with it.*

Being blindfolded or having the ears muffled seems to inhibit dowsing ability in many cases, while wearing a watch or being in a place where radio reception is poor tends to make the pendulum and rods erratic.

Practice is required to learn the rhythmical language of the pendulums, whose range of expression will be found to be much wider than a simple positive or negative; diagonal swings, half circles, pauses and oscillations all come to have a special meaning for the individual dowser. The ideal dowser (a rather rare and shy bird), does not need the pendulum or rod at all, ignores traditional dowsing measures like the 'Bishop's Rule' (a connection with pacing distances from the underground water and its depth) simply relying on the subtle burring and tingling in fingers or even feet, which act as direct instruments or perception. There are even clairvoyant dowsers, able to 'see' water or other things below the surface of the earth, and gauge, without any instrument save the human body, both depth, quantity and other remarkable facts.

*From *Elementary Radiesthesia and the Use of the Pendulum* by F.A. Archdale, published by The British Society of Dowsers.

Dowsing, or radiesthesia, is closely related to healing and would appear to employ the same psychic energies. These have nothing to do with the 'power of suggestion': if you try to use the will in healing work you will more than likely produce an opposite effect and the patient's condition will worsen. Radiesthesia has been a lifelong study for a number of highly gifted and skilled persons who have not been afraid to dedicate themselves to a science which continues to bear the stigma of unorthodoxy. Employing the techniques of dowsing, and linking the psychic energies to instruments which serve as interpreters – the 'Black Box' the Barraclough Triangle, and so on – medical radiesthesists have abundant proof that they are not dream pedlars. In particular, homeopathic medicine seems to work most efficiently when employed in conjunction with radiesthetic diagnosis and other psychic healing techniques.

Yet a great deal of healing goes on without conscious use of radiesthesia. The disciplines of what are generally called spiritual healing involve a sympathetic rapport with the patient, the healer's attention being upon the totality of the patient's being rather than the malfunction. I repeat, no effort of the will is involved: the healer simply tries to raise his own consciousness, and with it the consciousness of the patient, a state traditionally believed to be achieved by prayer, but in which neither creed nor formula are essential. Conviction is a prerequisite. The healer must be certain that all being forms an harmonious unity, that every manifestation of consciousness is ruled by Love and Law; that all we perceive is an expression of an incessant, intense cosmic creativity or pattern-making process whose periphery only we comprehend: that all creatures have the capacity to attain fullness and wholeness of being, and that the healer can here and now assist the practical realisation of this in his patient.

The above applies to the so-called spiritual healer: but again, there has to be an exchange of energies like those more exactly charted in radiesthesia: however, it is the worker's job to screw the bits together and set the rocket sailing into space, not to describe the way it is done.

Another kind of healer does the work through the agency of spirits, not by the use of magic, but through communication with entities on other frequencies of being, and employing the methods of spiritual healing described above in conjunction with mediumship or otherwise cooperating with spirit guides. The simpler and more shamanistic these kinds of healers are, the more they are misunderstood by observers. The so-called 'spirit surgeons' who operate in the Philippines have been widely criticised. Their use of bits of chicken liver or sheep's brain to reinforce the ritual impressiveness of their work meets with no understanding in sophisticated circles; they are dismissed as charlatans and do not have the intellectual equipment to answer the charges levelled against them. There is no doubt that they have had successful cures, and continue to do so. There is also no doubt that they have had failures. So do all healers. One of the greatest of modern healers, Harry Edwards, freely admits failures as well as triumphs – and curiously enough we sometimes fail when it seems terribly important that we should succeed, in the case of a loved one, for example, and immediately afterwards may succeed in curing the same condition in a stranger.

The question of the spirit surgeons, and their vulnerability to exploitation, is one which remains to be settled by enlightened, unprejudiced discussion. The arguments against healing, as with those against clairvoyance and any other form of psychic energy in action through the human agent, should not deter the beginner who feels drawn towards psychic activity of some kind. How often in my psychic work I have been told 'You did not foresee such-and-such', or 'Such-and-such never happened'. How often I have met with disappointment and failure! In psychic work we have no solid body of professional respectability and orthodoxy on which to lean in difficult times, and often we feel very much alone and defenceless in the face of intolerant incomprehension – scarcely, indeed, able to understand those curious forces which make us tick! That is part of the burden the full-time psychic must cheerfully shoulder, and carry on as best as he or she is able.

This little book's intent has been to show one or two ways by which psychism can be activated through employment of the intuition and imagination, and certainly through the positive energy released by wishing to do good. I have omitted to mention the use of Tarot and other cards, as these in turn open the door to related areas too complex to deal with in the allotted space.

Another study must deal with the use of the will or ego in ways related to psychic activity, and which are the mainsprings of magic. It is a field meriting much wider specialist investigation, but it is highly charged and extremely dangerous – not just for the practitioner, but for others. Elderly occidental magicians tend to be a psychic, physical and material mess, so hard to break are the habits of the Ego.

The patient reader is here and elsewhere seeking for attunement with Universal Being through widening the horizons of self-knowledge. Psychism is not out of place in the classroom, the laboratory, the workshop. For the elderly, the disabled, and those who lack sureness of direction, wandering hither and yon without confidence, awareness of psychic energy will open up a new, fascinating, land in which we are all pioneers . . . and yet where we are truly at home. To end with a paradox is good, for the paradox questions our stolid views about the real and the true.

I CHING NO. 22

PI Grace.

GRACE has success.
In small matters
It is favourable to
undertake something.

A GUIDE TO OCCULT BRITAIN

JOHN WILCOCK

MAKE YOUR OWN OCCULT ODYSSEY

'A pilgrimage to awaken lost memories, a journey to rediscover lost wisdom' – thus John Wilcock, traveller, occultist extraordinary and editor of the *Witches' Almanack*, describes his researches into the occult sites of Great Britain. Stonehenge, the Avebury Circle, Arthur's Seat above Edinburgh, Glastonbury, the Lligwy Burial Chamber on the Isle of Anglesey and the tumulus of Knowth are just a few of the ancient sites whose mystery John Wilcock revives in this unique guide, along with innumerable burial mounds, hill forts, fairy circles, green men and dragon carvings.

The author has designed his tour around five major routes which have been devised to take the mythologist, the occultist and the interested traveller through the maximum number of sites in any one area. With specific directions for easy access to each site, this is an invaluable guide for anyone interested in seeing for themselves the magic and mystery of occult Britain.

Occult/Cosmology   £1·25

0 7221 9140 5

THE SECRETS OF STONEHENGE

FERNAND NIEL

For thousands of years the awe-inspiring monoliths of Stonehenge have dared us to unlock their cosmic meaning. Now, in this revolutionary new book, Fernand Niel penetrates the mists of countless centuries to reveal astonishing facts about Stonehenge and the vanished tribe who built it.

Here is the lost knowledge that enabled Stonehenge's architects to transport the vast stone blocks over a hundred miles to the site; the startling links between those master-builders and the legendary cultures of Crete and Phoenicia; the meaning of the strange holes – some containing charred human remains – which encircle the monument; and the amazing discoveries which connect the stone circle with ages-old wellsprings of occult power such as the Pyramids and the Temple of Solomon.

SECRETS OF STONEHENGE is one of a series of fascinating investigations into the truth behind ancient mysteries.

Oceult/Cosmology   £1·25

0 7221 63797

A selection of Bestsellers from Sphere Books

TEMPLE DOGS	*Robert L. Duncan* 95p
THE PASSAGE	*Bruce Nicolaysen* 95p
CHARLIE IS MY DARLING	*Mollie Hardwick* £1.25
RAISE THE TITANIC!	*Clive Cussler* 95p
KRAMER'S WAR	*Derek Robinson* £1.25
THE CRASH OF '79	*Paul Erdman* £1.25
EMMA AND I	*Sheila Hocken* 85p
UNTIL THE COLOURS FADE	*Tim Jeal* £1.50
DR. JOLLY'S BOOK OF CHILDCARE	*Dr. Hugh Jolly* £1.95
MAJESTY	*Robert Lacey* £1.50
STAR WARS	*George Lucas* 95p
FALSTAFF	*Robert Nye* £1.50
EXIT SHERLOCK HOLMES	*Robert Lee Hall* 95p
THE MITTENWALD SYNDICATE	*Frederick Nolan* 95p
CLOSE ENCOUNTERS OF THE THIRD KIND	
	Steven Spielberg 85p
STAR FIRE	*Ingo Swann* £1.25
RUIN FROM THE AIR *Gordon Thomas & Max Morgan Witts* £1.50	
EBANO (Now filmed as ASHANTI) *Alberto Vazquez-Figueroa* 95p	
FIREFOX	*Craig Thomas* 95p

All Sphere books are available at your local bookshop or newsagent, or can be ordered direct from the address below. Just tick the titles you want and fill in the form below.

Name ....

Address ....

....

Write to Sphere Books, Cash Sales Department, P.O. Box 11, Falmouth, Cornwall TR10 9EN

Please enclose cheque or postal order to the value of the cover price plus:

UK: 22p for the first book plus 10p per copy for each additional book ordered to a maximum charge of 82p

OVERSEAS: 30p for the first book and 10p for each additional book

BFPO & EIRE: 22p for the first book plus 10p per copy for the next 6 books, thereafter 4p per book

Sphere Books reserve the right to show new retail prices on covers which may differ from those previously advertised in the text or elsewhere, and to increase postal rates in accordance with the GPO